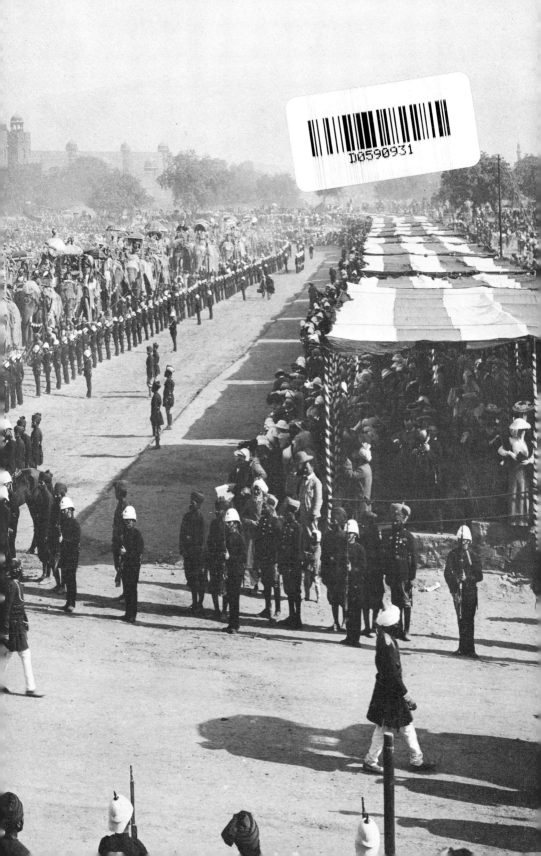

The Victorian Empire

(*endpapers*) Imperial pomp. The
Viceroy's state entry into Delhi
during the 1903 Durbar.

1837-1901

The Victorian Empire

A PICTORIAL HISTORY

DENIS JUDD

Weidenfeld & Nicolson

5 Winsley Street London W1

To
Dorothy,
Katie,
Luke and
Benjamin,
who all
enjoy looking at
pictures

Designed by Shashi Rawal for
George Weidenfeld & Nicolson Ltd, London

Photoset in Great Britain by
BAS Printers Limited,
Over Wallop, Hampshire

Printed by Unwin Brothers Ltd.
The Gresham Press, Old Woking, Surrey, England.
A member of the Staples Printing Group.

SBN 297 00102 7

Contents

Photographic acknowledgments 6

Preface 7

Introduction 8

PART ONE
The Rising of the Sun 1837-1870

1 Canada: the eldest daughter 16

2 Colonies in the antipodes 30

3 Briton and Boer 54

4 India; an Empire in the Making 68

5 Scattered Possessions 94

PART TWO
The Sun at Its Zenith 1870-1901

6 Imperial Order and Disorder 114

7 The Emergence of the Dominions 128

8 Southern Africa 1870–1907 146

9 The Raj in India 1870–1905 164

10 Egypt and the Sudan 184

11 The Scramble for Empire 202

Epilogue 215

Bibliography 217

Index 220

Photographic acknowledgments

The photographs in this book are reproduced by the kind permission of the following.

Australian High Commission: 30: 36: 40/1: 40/2: 137: 141: 142: Associated Newspapers: 123: British Museum: 8/1: 8/3: 8/4: 8/5: 8/6: 14: 201: Canadian High Commission (Courtesy of the Public Archives of Canada): 17: 18: 19/1: 19/2: 25/2: 29: 131: 135/1: 135/2: Canadian Pacific Railway Company Limited: 128-9: Church Missionary Society: 96/1: 97: 106/1: 106/2: 177: 210/2: Commonwealth Office Library: 20: 22: 23: 26/1: 26/2: 28: 37: 38: 44: 67: 94/2: 100: 104: 117/1: 118: 124: 136: 146/1: 151: 152: 159/1: 159/2: 160: 162: 204: 207: 208: 209: 210/1: 213: De Beers Consolidated Mines Ltd: 146/2: 148: 150: Delhi Sketch Book: 77: J. R. Freeman: 20: 22: 23: 26/1: 26/2: 28: 37: 38: 44: 67: 77: 94/2: 100: 104: 117/1: 118: 124: 136: 146/1: 151: 152: 159/1: 159/2: 160: 162: 204: 207: 208: 209: 210/1: 213: India Office Library: 72-3: 74: 76/1: 76/2: 78: 79: 81: 86: 87: 88-9/2: 92: 167/2: 174: 175/1: 175/2: 176: 178: 179: 181: 183: Mansell Collection: 25/1: 35/1: 35/2: 43: 54: 59: 60-1: 62: 66: 70: 71: 80: 82-3: 84: 85: 88-9/1: 90: 94/1: 96/2: 99: 107/1: 107/2: 109: 110: 113: 114: 117/2: 120-1: 127: 132: 138: 149: 163: 166-7: 169/1: 169/2: 172: 173/1: 184: 189: 191: 193: 196: 198/1: 198/2: 200: 212: Mary Evans Picture Library: 48: 94-5: 116: 167/1: 187: 202: National Army Museum, Camberley: 173/2: New Zealand High Commission: 45: 47/1: 47/2: 51: 52-3: 64: 144: Punch: 119: Radio Times Hulton Picture Library: 32-3: 103: 108: 111: 153: 156: 157: 164: 190: 205/1: 205/2: 211: South African Embassy: 56-7: 154/1: 154/2: 158: 161.

Jacket photographs: front by courtesy of John Curtis: back by courtesy of Michael Raeburn. The maps are by Design Practitioners Ltd.

Preface

THIS BOOK attempts to capture the substance of a vanished epoch. The Victorian Empire now seems almost as remote from our experience as the Age of Chivalry or the Glorious Revolution. There are still some alive who recall Joseph Chamberlain at the Colonial Office or who marched with Roberts to Pretoria – but they are not many. The bones of the great Empire-builders lie in the dust along with those of their critics and opponents. The flags that flew over Cawnpore and Ladysmith are faded now, and will never be raised again.

From the distance of seventy years it is both instructive and profitable to appraise Queen Victoria's Empire with an objective eye; to be aware of its magnificence and its squalor, to recall its high ideals and its arrogant assumptions. In this way, aided by the enormous scholastic output of the last few decades as well as by the evidence of the camera, we can achieve a valuable perspective.

DENIS JUDD
London 1970

Introduction

THE YOUNG Queen Victoria ascended the throne during an era of outstanding change in British colonial policy. The great Whig majority in the newly reformed Parliament had abolished slavery throughout the Empire in 1833. The Commons' Aborigines Committee of 1837 had laid down principles, enlightened enough for the times, by which non-European peoples within the Empire should be treated. The Radical Imperialists pressed, with increasing success, for the constructive handling of the under-populated settlement colonies. Wakefield's schemes for systematic colonisation were put into imperfect practice in the Antipodes, and Lord Durham produced in 1839 his classical recommendation of responsible government for the two Canadas.

While statesmen and colonial theorists restructured imperial policies, the British working man emigrated in hundreds of thousands. Between 1831 and 1871 5,932,000 emigrants left Great Britain. The overwhelming majority made for North America, Australia and New Zealand; a few thousand only settled in the Cape or Natal. This gigantic emigration not only added substantial numbers to the population of the United States, but guaranteed that Canada and Australasia would be dominated for the foreseeable future by English-speaking people. The average emigrant probably knew little and cared less for the Aborigines Committee or the notion of imperial trusteeship, but by blazing into Ontario, or South Australia, or Otago, he was shaping the Empire as surely as any policy-maker.

Imperial unity through the Post Office. The stamps for the Cape, India, New South Wales, Barbados and New Zealand were first issued during the 1850's. The Newfoundland stamp shows Victoria at the end of her reign.

9

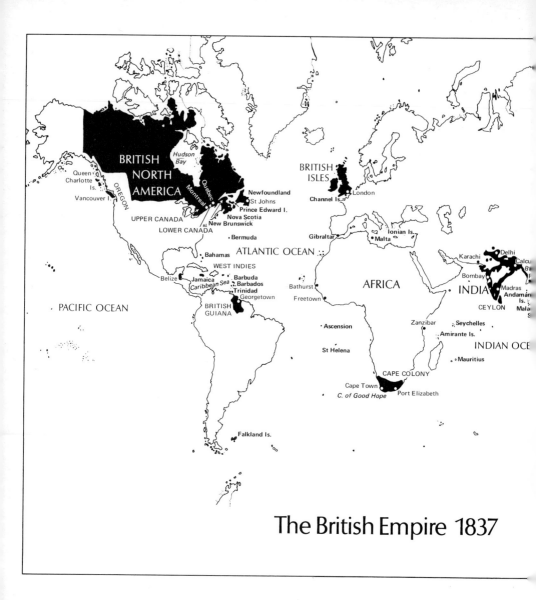

The British Empire 1837

At home the irresistible progress of the industrial revolution swept away the lifeless system of imperial protection. Industrialists and workers wanted cheap bread, stable prices, worthwhile wages. Under the strain of the 1845 potato famine and the agitation of the Anti-Corn Law League, Robert Peel sacrificed the privileged fiscal position of home-grown wheat in 1846. Peel's decision broke the Tory party in two, but inaugurated the system of free trade. In 1849 the Corn Laws were finally scrapped and the remaining Navigation Acts repealed. The sugar duties followed them

into oblivion, and by 1853 all imperial preferences had vanished.

The ending of protection made easier the wholesale grant of responsible government to the settlement colonies. By the end of the 1850's self-government had been achieved in the Canadian Union and in all the eastern North American colonies; in New South Wales, Victoria, Queensland, Tasmania, South Australia, and New Zealand; the Cape and British Columbia were set on the same path. This devolution of responsibility gladdened alike the hearts of Cobdenite Radicals, Benthamites, Whigs, and many Tories. To be sure, the Royal Navy was still the guarantor of imperial security, and paid for by the British government, but local defence could be placed increasingly in colonial hands.

Apart from the untidy and traumatic events of the 1857 Indian Mutiny, and the embarrassing repercussions of the Jamaica Rebellion of 1865, the mid-Victorian Empire could get on with business as usual and a fair return on investment. Often humanitarian sensibilities and a 5% dividend went hand in hand, a state of affairs as satisfying for the conscience as for the pocket. Moral suasion and the Royal Navy's guns kept a host of princelings and sultans obedient to British advice and their territories open to British exports.

The aims of colonial policy were essentially modest, and the methods of achieving them appropriately pragmatic. The nation's energies were chiefly expended elsewhere; in making political and social adjustments to industrial development, and in buying in the cheapest market and selling in the most profitable. The confidence that progress would be achieved was based as much on a booming export trade as on the great instruments of Victorian reform.

By contrast, the late-Victorians seemed dedicated imperialists. The Conservative party provided the political backbone of the imperialist cause, aided after 1892 by the demoniac energies of the lapsed Radical Joseph Chamberlain. The Empire had become respectable; imperialism a sanctified philosophy. Even the Liberal party tried to come to terms with these new enthusiasms, and a substantial section, led by such glittering younger spirits as Rosebery, Asquith, Grey and Haldane, became known as the Liberal-Imperialists. Gladstonian Liberals, Radicals, and Labour men might shun such posturing, but the Liberal-Imperialists looked set fair to inherit the party's future.

The clamour and strident sentiment that attended the imperialism of the 1890's convinced both critics and supporters of Empire that unprecedented forces were at work. It became fashionable to discern a 'New Imperialism', and to define its salient characteristics. The jingoism of the music halls, and the literary and journalistic excesses of imperial devotees, grew as Matabele and dervish went down before the maxim guns. The competition for colonies in Africa and the deepening crisis in the Transvaal lent an unusual excitement to routine political manoeuvring. After 1896 the development of a cheap popular press, that could present great events for the digestion of the barely literate masses, fed countless starved imaginations.

The Victorian proletariat had been herded into factories and workshops, subjected to industrial regulation, and denied the fullest political freedoms. It was hardly surprising that many of them should have gloried at the red-coated infantry marching into Kumasi, or at the steel shield that the Royal Navy flung across the oceans. In this sense, imperialist sentiment was merely an inflated patriotism. It is also tempting to see symptoms of national insecurity on the other side of the jingo penny. In the 1890's Great Britain, for all her territorial pomp and splendour, was without allies and openly detested by many in Europe and the United States. 'Splendid Isolation' was in fact uncomfortable and costly; a rationalisation of a predicament, not a calculated policy. Thus in the public exultations over the triumph at Omdurman or at the relief of Mafeking can be seen the reactions of an uncertain people.

Belief in Britain's imperial mission included the assumption that the Anglo-Saxon race embodied virtues denied to less fortunate members of mankind. Britain and her settlement colonies, therefore, belonged to an English-speaking confederacy devoted not only to self-interest but to the loftier ideals of personal freedom and stable political institutions. Despite the embarrassing activities of the Irish Fenians, the United States was considered part of this international freemasonry;

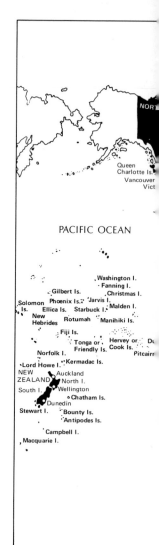

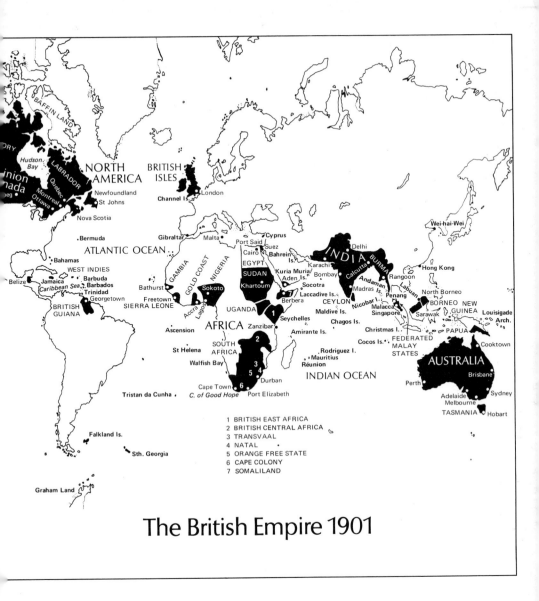

The British Empire 1901

1 BRITISH EAST AFRICA
2 BRITISH CENTRAL AFRICA
3 TRANSVAAL
4 NATAL
5 ORANGE FREE STATE
6 CAPE COLONY
7 SOMALILAND

Imperial Germany was an immature but successful affiliated member. The subject peoples of the British Empire were, on this analysis, being ruled for their own good by benevolent and gifted overseers.

The economic justifications for empire were enthusiastically reinterpreted towards the end of the century. Talk of surplus capital, over-production, trade following the flag, endorsed the new territorial acquisitions in Africa. Partly this was a restatement of the conviction that successful commerce was Britain's truest interest; partly it was a reaction to the post-1870 economic

13

depressions and to fiercer competition from abroad. At any rate, Rhodes in Africa, and Joseph Chamberlain at home were able to advocate expansion on the grounds of trade advantages. Chamberlain in particular painted an attractive prospect of the profitable use of under-developed imperial estates, and his undoubted appeal to the working classes relied heavily upon the questionable equation between imperial possession and domestic prosperity.

From the 1880's there was serious consideration of the reorganisation of the white-settled Empire. Imperial federation, a more unified imperial defence system, preferential tariffs within the Empire, were seen as practical possibilities. Colonial Conferences discussed these proposals, and Joseph Chamberlain advocated each of them to a greater or lesser degree. By 1901, however, little had been achieved. The self-governing colonies were jealous of their status and chary of sub-ordination in grand-sounding schemes of imperial cooperation. Voluntary and informal support for the Mother Country were clearly preferable to rigid prior commitments.

Nor should it be supposed that the ideal of Empire was universally acceptable at home. The average Englishmen must have had a hazy picture of the finer points of imperial responsibility and endeavour. There were, moreover, many dogged and well-informed critics of the 'New Imperialism'. The capitalist drive behind many annexations, the activities of organisations like Rhodes' British South Africa Company (accused by the *Investors' Chronicle* in 1894 of swindling its share-holders), the braggart militarism, the manifestations of racial arrogance, were all the subject of bitter attack in Parliament and throughout the country. Set beside the urgent need for social reform in Britain, extravagant imperial attitudes seemed at best irrelevant and at worst callous and indifferent.

The disastrously prosecuted Boer War of 1899–1902 provided the critics of Empire with a superabundance of ammunition. Events in South Africa also pricked the grossly inflated imperialist bubble and restored a certain sobriety and perspective to the pursuit of imperial policy. In the election of 1906 the Liberals were swept to their last great victory and annihilated the party that had presided over the frenzy of *fin de siècle* imperialism. The 'New Imperialism' was shown to be hollow and largely meaningless. Although it had not lacked brilliant propagandists, it was essentially a brash cover for an altered set of national priorities. In Africa it is even arguable that the 'New Imperialism' was chiefly the means of defending the old Empire east of Suez.

Nonetheless the last years of the Victorian age did see the Empire at its zenith. Almost a quarter of mankind lived beneath the Union Jack, a quarter of the globe was painted red. The Empire encompassed every climate, and an astounding variety of humanity lived within its borders. It was, of course, the *British* Empire, yet in some ways it was anything but British. Barely twelve per cent of its citizens were European, let alone British. Its most commonly practised religions were Hinduism and Islam, not Christianity. British administration had hardly penetrated the hinterlands of newly acquired colonies in Africa or the Pacific. The Empire was the object of both overflowing pride and downright opposition. Yet although it could claim nearly three centuries of history, and seemed to promise a solid future, it was little more than fifty years from collapse and total disintegration. In 1901 the prospect of so rapid a fall would have dumbfounded imperialists and anti-imperialists alike.

Sir Sandford Fleming's 'Beaver' stamp for the Union of Canada was printed in New York and issued in 1851, sixteen years before Canadian federation.

1 Canada: the eldest daughter

Anglo-French rivalry; the civil disturbances of 1837; the Durham Report and the 1840 Act of Union; a pioneer society, and the influx of immigrants; the development of responsible government and fiscal autonomy; the federation of 1867; the first Dominion.

BY 1837 BRITISH NORTH AMERICA had shrunk to a moderate measure. Following the loss of the thirteen rebellious colonies, the British crown ruled Quebec, Ontario, Nova Scotia, New Brunswick and Newfoundland. While none of these provinces were as yet particularly valuable commercially nor of vital strategic significance, they were nonetheless the most senior of the colonies of white settlement. This seniority sprang both from the long history of Quebec and from the lengthy association of Britain with the North American mainland.

At the end of the Seven Years War in 1763 France had surrendered all her territory in Canada. The American Revolution had provided Ontario and the Maritimes with several thousand dispossessed United Empire loyalists. Although dedicated anti-republicans, the loyalists were used to the practice of representative institutions. Chiefly to placate these new citizens, although also to contain the animosities of the French settlers, Britain in 1791 divided Canada into an Upper and a Lower province and provided both with a reasonably liberal constitution.

This division, however, could not be permanent. The attempt to balance English-speaking and French-speaking factions broke down. The numbers of English Canadians were increased by steady immigration from the homeland; French Canada received few such reinforcements. By the 1830's it seemed inevitable that Canada's future lay in the supremacy of its English-speaking people. They in turn chafed at their now

English-speaking rebels drilling in North York, Ontario in Autumn 1837.

inadequate political institutions. Some turned their eyes on the unfolding might of the United States and prepared for the absorption of Canada by its expanding neighbour. Others pointed to the recent rebellion of Spain's South American colonies. In Lower Canada Papineau voiced the shrill grievances of Quebec separatism. From London it looked as if Canada was set for independence.

These prophesies were reinforced in 1837 by rebellions in Upper and Lower Canada. The year of the young Victoria's accession to the throne saw both her English and French-speaking subjects in revolt. If Canada, with its population of one and a half million, broke away, what was to stop the citizens of New South Wales or the Cape from following suit?

As it happened, nothing of the sort occurred. The 'rebellions' of 1837 were little short of military farces, and their far more serious political implications were brilliantly countered. Lord Melbourne's government dispatched Lord Durham to report on the disturbances, and in so doing commissioned one of the classical statements of British colonial policy. Not that the motives for choosing Durham were so high-minded. With his radical convictions, enormous personal wealth, and rigorous standards, Durham was an awkward colleague for the easy-going Melbourne and the cautious Lord John Russell. Three thousand miles of ocean would render 'Radical Jack' more agreeable.

To aid him in his mission Durham took two vigorous and constructive minds – Edward Gibbon Wakefield and Charles Buller, both colonial theorists of the first rank. But he was also armed with his own keen perception and his capacity for confident analysis. These were qualities ideally suited to the task in Canada. The Durham Report was issued in 1839, by which time its author was a dying man. Its sweep, clarity and daring were an appropriate epitaph.

Durham's chief recommendation was that responsible government should be extended to Canada. This was in itself a revolutionary suggestion. Hitherto representative government had been the most advanced form of British colonial constitution – with Governor and Executive Council balanced against a Legislature which

Louis Joseph Papineau (1786–1871). Papineau gave eloquent utterance to the separatist and republican convictions of Quebec.

Left: Battle of St Eustache, 1837. French rebels confront British regulars and Canadian volunteers. About seventy rebels were killed.

Right: Lord Durham. His Report, issued in 1839, pointed the way towards responsible government for Canada.

was part nominated, part elected. Durham dismissed this system with the words 'it may fairly be said that the natural state of government in all [our North American Provinces] is that of collision between the executive and the representative body'.

Durham envisaged that responsible government would rest on the assumption that the elected members of the Legislature could be trusted to form an administration. The Governor would play a part similar to that of a constitutional monarch. The ministers would be ultimately *responsible* to the Legislature or Assembly. The authority of the Crown would be enshrined in the Governor's position, although Whitehall should make it a practice never to interfere through the Governor in domestic colonial issues. On the other hand, matters of Imperial concern (such as constitutional amendment, foreign and commercial relations, and the disposal of public lands) should be reserved for the discretion of the British government.

These constitutional proposals were only part of the famous Report. In addition, Durham recommended union between Upper and Lower Canada. This measure seemed best suited to guarantee the political domination of the English-speaking majority in the long term. Although Durham was rapturously received in Quebec, and was determined to maintain French majority rule

in Lower Canada, he had no doubts as to the appropriate future course of Canadian national development. Quite simply, Durham believed that Anglo-Saxon society was more dynamic and progressive than French society. He advocated, therefore, the cultural absorption of French Canadians by English-speaking Canadians. There was some justification for this attitude. Quebec, with its lingering heritage from the *ancien régime*, hardly seemed to guarantee progress, and the virtues of its citizens, though undeniably solid, had little in common with Durham's own vivid convictions.

To this optimistic, if somewhat arrogant, belief in the superiority of Anglo-Saxon institutions and abilities, Durham added another. This was his conviction that if the Canadian constitution was altered as he suggested, then political separation between Britain and Canada might well be avoided. To many contemporaries this was almost as revolutionary a concept as the proposal to establish responsible government. The transformation of the white-settled Empire into independent republics was confidently predicted by Cobdenite Radicals and high Tories alike. The prospect was indeed welcome to many since it was assumed (from the example of the United States) that political independence would not mean commercial and cultural severance as well.

In the event, Durham's contention was both right and wrong. Although the colonies of white settlement did not formally secede from the Empire, the long-term implication of responsible government could only be independent sovereignty. In other respects the Report was applied as the Melbourne administration thought fit. Union was enacted in 1840, though without the degree of responsible government so central to Durham's

Her Majesty's men o'war *Charybidis*, *Stellite* and *Cameleon* at anchor in Esquimault harbour, Victoria Island, 1867.

recommendations. But although the future seemed to belong to English-speaking Canadians, Quebec remained an undigested lump in the gullet of Anglo-Saxon society.

As yet, of course, Canadian society in general was raw and ill-formed. There were, to be sure, the old settled areas from Nova Scotia to Ontario, and cities like Montreal and Toronto offered not only urban amenities but something of a cultural standard. In the main, however, life was hard, and life on the frontiers, in particular, uncertain.

Canada was overwhelmingly rural, and in the countryside brick or stonebuilt houses were rare exceptions. Although on the shores of the Great Lakes the climate was kinder and wheat grew well, elsewhere the environment was harsh and sometimes savage. The long winters limited agricultural activity and cut communications. Not that there were many means of communication to cut. Roads were few and far between, and even when they existed were mostly made of dirt. In summer the roads covered travellers with dust, in winter they not infrequently became quagmires. The railroads were sparser than the roads and in any case geared to the movement of freight rather than the transportation of people.

The Canadian settler faced a life of unremitting toil. His womenfolk could, in addition, expect frequent pregnancies and hazardous child-bearing. Professional medical assistance was often not available and amateurish folklore and experiment were not acceptable substitutes. The horse and buggy were among the most luxurious forms of travel, and the vast bulk of farming was done by hand, with scythe and sickle, not by mechanical reaper. Isolation rendered the homestead more self-sufficient. Frequently pioneer expansion outstripped the ministrations of organised religion. More important, perhaps, new communities were not uncommonly without the rule of law.

Canadian society in 1840 was characterised, therefore, by activity and labour, if by little culture. There was not much domestic manufacturing and newspapers were hard to come by. Yet amid all this austerity and toil there existed hope; the chance of a better life, the prospect of becoming a cattle baron or a timber

Log-cabin society. Trader McPherson and family. Marriages between frontiersmen and Indian women were by no means uncommon.

magnate. This, above all, explains the increase in Canada's population from an estimated 350,000 in 1815 to close on 4,000,000 by 1867.

In Britain the 'hungry forties' caused hundreds of thousands to emigrate. In the years 1841–6 about 689,000 left the United Kingdom. Although most of these made for the United States, about 246,000 landed in Canada. From 1847 to 1854, however, this flow became a flood. Not only was there steady agricultural depression in England and heavy periodical industrial unemployment, but in 1845 potato famine and harvest failure hit much of Europe. Famine affected no country worse than Ireland, which had a greater density of population per acre of cultivated land than any other in Europe. Relief measures were at best palliative. Starvation faced literally millions of people. The mid-nineteenth-century state had no sophisticated welfare schemes. The British government's crude response to the disasters of 1845–7 was to encourage emigration and, reluctantly, to defray some of the expense. This at least kept intact the widely accepted belief that prudence and self-reliance were supreme virtues.

A tidal wave of immigrants struck the New World: the Irish, of course, and destitute Englishmen, but also

The original inhabitants. A Sioux Indian encampment near the border with the United States.

tens of thousands of Scottish Highlanders for whom the century since the catastrophe of Culloden Moor had been one of eviction, persecution and hunger. While this mass exodus, combined with a revival of British industry during the Crimean War of 1854–6, depleted the numbers of unemployed, it created problems on the other side of the Atlantic. The Irish beggars who had flocked down the lanes and highways of England were scarcely more welcome in Upper and Lower Canada. Emigrant ships were frequently packed to the scuppers; insanitary, unventilated breeding grounds for disease and personal degradation. Thousands died in conditions hardly superior to those of a slave ship on the middle passage.

Many citizens of Montreal and Toronto looked with distaste upon this pestilential, illiterate horde. In the immediate aftermath of the great Irish famine of 1845, 6,000 orphan children of deceased Irish parents were to be found in Montreal alone. Although the British government eventually agreed in 1848 to pay for the cost of transporting the immigrants across the Atlantic, the burden of local relief fell upon Canada. The ill-feeling generated by these events was only partly offset by the realisation that a substantial number of new citizens had been gained.

While the immigrants set about the task of building a new life, the government of Canada underwent significant change. The decade following the Durham Report resolved some of the problems left in the air by the 1840 Act of Union. At first the omens were not propitious. Governors-General such as Lord Sydenham acted more like George III than as a constitutional monarch. There were, admittedly, justifications for such heavy-handed manipulation. Could the French be trusted to play the correct political game? In addition, the early 1840's were marked by diplomatic confrontations between Britain and the United States. Although the New Brunswick-Maine border dispute was amicably settled in 1842, there was continuing bickering over the partition of Oregon and rivalry for control of the proposed Panama Canal.

Not until 1846 did matters improve. Oregon was divided; the north becoming British Columbia, the south United States territory. The advent of the constructive Earl Grey to the War and Colonial Office meant that real responsible government for Canada would follow shortly. The appointment of Durham's son-in-law Lord Elgin as the Canadian Governor-General was equally promising. Elgin believed that the French could be trusted, and was on one occasion pelted in his state coach by incensed if misguided English loyalists. His crime was to support, and be prepared to sign, a Bill compensating French citizens for losses sustained to their property during the disturbance of 1837. To Sir Allan McNab and the loyalists these concessions smacked of treachery. In fact, such impartial treatment was the only genuine basis for responsible government.

In 1848 Nova Scotia was given responsible government. The Canadian Union soon followed suit. By 1855 all of the eastern colonies had become self-governing, and a year later Vancouver Island and British Columbia seemed set on the same path. To many contemporaries these developments, paralleled as they were by similar advances in the Australasian colonies, seemed the inevitable prelude to full independence from Britain. The ripe colonial apples were about to fall from the parental tree. Since Britain had by 1849 abandoned the system of commercial protection which had hitherto

Moose-hunting scene, 1868. Trappers and huntsmen could reap handsome profits.

Fire in the land of snow. Prairie fires were a common threat to crops and livestock.

bound the component parts of the Empire together, the secession of the settlement colonies was perfectly compatible with fiscal policy. With the Corn Laws and the Navigation Acts scrapped, British manufacturers could turn with full vigour to the markets of the whole world rather than to the markets of the Empire.

The coming of free trade, however, posed certain problems. From the colonial point of view it might well be desirable to establish nationally advantageous tariffs. Canada blazed a trail through this speculative territory. In 1854 the government of Canada concluded a reciprocal commercial treaty with the United States, even though ratification depended upon the approval of the crown and the British Parliament. The next step was even more revolutionary. In 1859 Galt, the Canadian Finance Minister, imposed a tariff on steel from other parts of the Empire. While a tariff designed to raise revenue was just within the limits of orthodoxy, Galt chose not to rely on such casuistry. The tariff, he insisted, was to protect Canadian industry, and if the British government were prepared to block the measure they must also be prepared to administer the colony against the wishes of its inhabitants.

These arguments were conclusive. British ministers and Sheffield steel masters swallowed their objections and conceded. The day had been won not by the threat of independence but by that of greater *dependence*. Times had changed indeed. As it happened, the British concession was altogether fruitful. Canada showed no real desire to sever her connection with the crown, and British steel exports to the colony continued to increase.

Above: Solid if unsophisticated. An early customs house in British Columbia.

Left: Colonial hotel, Fraser River, on the waggon trail through British Columbia, 1867.

By the 1860's a number of factors caused Canadians to consider the desirability of federation. The union of Upper and Lower Canada seemed only a partial answer to problems common to the Maritimes and British Columbia, as well as to the new territories being opened up in between. At first sight, however, the differences between these colonies were more marked than the similarities. Newfoundland was detached from the mainland. The Maritimes (Nova Scotia, New Brunswick and Prince Edward Island) were hundreds of miles from Quebec and Ontario. From Ontario to the Rocky Mountains swept the vast but barely populated prairies. Vancouver Island and British Columbia clung to the Pacific coast three and a half thousand miles from St John's, Newfoundland. A large portion of British North America, from the northern wastelands to the foothills of the Rockies was, in any case, ruled by the Hudson Bay Company.

Provincialism was strong. The antipathy of Quebec militants for Ontario Tories was not unique. There was little natural harmony between Newfoundland fishermen and Toronto bankers, or between Montrealers and the lumberjacks of British Columbia. It could indeed be argued that the obvious economic unities were not east-west but north-south, across the border with the United States. New Brunswick and Maine, Ontario and Michigan, British Columbia and Washington had much more in common than shared boundaries.

It was not, however, to be the manifest destiny of the United States to swallow Canada. One reason for this lay in the fears generated by the expansionist vigour of the Republic which had in 1848 stripped Mexico of thousands of square miles of territory, including California. In the early 1860's the bitter and costly war to preserve the Union made absorption by the United States an unattractive prospect. Nor did the Irish-Fenian raids across the border reassure Canadians whose first loyalty was to the British crown.

In these circumstances, both British and Canadian statesmen looked to some form of union. The creation of a state able to resist both the diplomatic and economic domination of the American Republic was the ideal to be achieved. Once established, a united Canada could hope for better credit and a recognisable

place among the nations of the world. Although this would not resolve the problem of identity, it would lend some coherence to a country set in North America while retaining strong links with Britain and containing a large French minority. Doubtless, growing American hostility to the 1854 reciprocal trade treaty and British offers of financial assistance for the projected inter-colonial railway were powerful incentives. So too was the advocacy of the Tory John Macdonald and the Radical George Brown of Ontario, of George Cartier of Quebec, and of Edward Watkins, director of the Hudson Bay Company.

The formal initiative came, appropriately enough, from Nova Scotia, New Brunswick and Prince Edward Island. These provinces, while discussing a scheme for their own union, proposed that the principle should be extended to include the whole of British North America. A conference at Quebec in 1865 approved federation, and in 1867 the British Parliament passed the British North America Act. The first Dominion had emerged.

The chief characteristic of the new constitution was strong central government combined with reassuring concessions to provincialism – essential in the case of Quebec. British constitutional models prevailed over those of the United States, perhaps because Canadian leaders had seen at close quarters the bloody failings of American federalism. The Dominion government, at the new capital of Ottawa, was to consist of a Gover-nor-General appointed by the British monarch, an elected Lower and a nominated Upper House, a ministry responsible to the elected chamber, and an independent judiciary.

The provinces were each to have a Lieutenant-Governor, and a legislature and administration which were in effect carried over from pre-federation days. They were given specifically defined authority over matters such as education, agriculture, and immigration. Quebec was also guaranteed a minimum of sixty-five seats in the Canadian House of Commons. In all spheres of governmental activity not enumerated by the 1867 Act the administration at Ottawa was to be supreme. Amendments to the constitution were to rest with the Parliament at Westminster.

Despite a certain amount of subsequent provincial wriggling, the new constitution worked. It is true that legal haggling over the rights of provincial governments provided Ottawa with some frustration, but the federation itself was capable of surviving such activities intact. Most important of all was the fact that the new Dominion had grown from Canadian initiatives, not from British pressures. Yet the end-product (tedious though most M.P.'s at Westminster found the debates on the 1867 Act) could only be fundamentally satisfying for Britain.

Not all the provinces of Canada joined the federation in 1867. Prince Edward Island stayed out until 1873, Newfoundland until 1949. The original members were Upper and Lower Canada, Nova Scotia and New Brunswick. As the great inter-colonial railway crept westwards new territories were opened up, and the federation grew. The trans-continental railway was to be the string upon which the beads of Canadian unity were to hang. In 1867 this necklace, though incomplete, was well-ordered and some of the beads at least shone like jewels.

The making of the nation. Confederation Convention at Charlottetown, Prince Edward Island, 1864. John A. MacDonald, a future Canadian Prime Minister, is in the centre, sitting on the steps.

2　Colonies in the Antipodes

AUSTRALIA: *early settlement and the transportation of convicts; Wakefield and experiments in establishing colonies; the great gold rush and the battle of the Eureka stockade; blackfellows, squatters and bushrangers; the movement towards responsible self-government.*

NEW ZEALAND: *the New Zealand Company and the British annexation of 1840; confrontation with the Maoris and the Treaty of Waitangi; the Maori Wars; gold rush and agricultural boom; growth of responsible government and the problem of the Maori franchise.*

AUSTRALIA　COOK'S VOYAGE in 1770 to the fertile and attractive eastern coast of Australia came at an opportune time. Despite Dutch exploration of western and southern Australia in the seventeenth century, the vast new continent remained untenanted save for the scattered tribes of the indigenous aborigines. The Dutch, secure in their monopoly of the East Indies' spices, had little time for an apparently barren land devoid of profitable trade. When, therefore, the loss of the American colonies deprived Britain of her traditional dumping ground for convicts and undesirables it was easy to turn to Australia instead.

In 1788 Governor Phillip landed with troops and the first batch of convicts at Botany Bay. From this settlement grew the port of Sydney and the colony of New South Wales. Although Phillip had requested that free settlers with some knowledge of farming should also be sent out, by 1800 only twenty or so had materialised. The convicts, however, continued to arrive. By 1792 it seemed as if the settlement, with its population of 3,000 and its newly cultivated land, could survive. This did not mean that Botany Bay and its hinterland were attractive to the eye, and in April 1790 a British officer complained that 'The country . . . is past all dispute a

Governor Davey's Pictorial Proclamation to the Aborigines, 1816. Unfortunately, the egalitarian principles illustrated were not always adhered to.

31

wretched one.' But, as William Pitt informed the House of Commons in 1791, 'No cheaper mode of disposing of convicts could be found.'

The transportation of convicts continued until the first years of Victoria's reign. When in 1840 the system was ended in New South Wales it had left a harsh mark upon Australian development. Although in New South Wales, Van Dieman's Land (Tasmania) and Western Australia the convicts provided an essential source of very cheap labour, transportation had aroused fierce controversy in England and Australia.

In the new colonies, convicts were frequently accused of debauching moral standards and encouraging vice. This argument was difficult to sustain while convicts were herded together into barracks and labour camps. A substantial number, however, were assigned to settlers as servants or, when on remission, allowed to

Bound for Botany Bay. Convicts on their way to the penal settlements.

live in private lodgings. If, in these circumstances, recourse was had to Sydney prostitutes or hard liquor, it was hardly surprising. In any case, employers were mostly prepared to overlook such alleged delinquencies in return for the higher profits accruing from cheap convict labour. In 1840 there were 56,000 transportees in New South Wales and Van Dieman's Land working out their sentences.

The supporters of transportation were not confined to Australian employers. In England it was argued that the convicts were at least removed from a society characterised by low wages and severe unemployment. Certainly very few convicts returned home after serving their sentences. The new land did seem to offer greater opportunities and more substantial freedoms. The high cost of the passage back may have deterred many, but even those who had not achieved the prosperity of Magwitch in *Great Expectations* frequently preferred their new country to the old.

Against this could be set the contention that free immigration was inhibited by the transportation system. It was not merely that free labourers found themselves undercut, but that a society which relied so heavily upon a convict population was not considered fit for women and children. It is undeniably true that, at least until 1840, the overwhelming proportion of emigrants from Britain chose to cross the Atlantic rather than venture to the South Seas. These would-be immigrants were apparently not convinced by the reformist claim that many convicts were spiritually saved by transportation. The Anglican church and later the Catholics made staunch efforts to improve and uplift. The transport ships were loaded with bibles, prayer books and tracts, and the convicts' reading matter included such cautionary works as *Exercises Against Lying*, *Exhortations to Chastity* and *Dissuasions From Stealing*.

Once in the penal settlements there was often no alternative to chastity and not much to steal. The churches, however, continued with compulsory services. The Anglicans, being effectively the established church, were also involved in early educational endeavours. But the large numbers of Irish transported in the first fifty years of Australian development gave the Catholic church a role out of proportion to its contemporary functions in England or even in the United States. A Roman Catholic see was established in 1835, and government assistance was extended to all religious bodies for church building, ecclesiastical salaries and the like.

Although the great majority of convicts came from the industrial slums of England and were transported (at least after 1815) for fairly serious crimes, there were clear exceptions to this pattern. Most remarkable, though few in number, were political offenders. These included the legendary Tolpuddle Martyrs of 1834, as well as some Chartists, and some rebels from the Canadian disturbances of 1837. In addition, the persistent unrest and occasionally violent political crises in Ireland resulted in quite heavy transportations. The apparently savage sentences passed on Irishmen who had disobeyed curfew often reflected the law's opinion that the victims had been involved in clandestine and seditious political activities.

If Radicals in England tended to deplore transportation, they were strong advocates of well-organised free settlement. Chief among such theorists was Edward Gibbon Wakefield. While languishing in Newgate prison for abducting an heiress (twice, as it happened), Wakefield composed his plan for the systematic colonisation of Australasia. Under the somewhat misleading title of *A Letter from Sydney*, he argued that successful colonisation depended upon achieving a harmony between capital and labour, and between the various classes of a settler society. Wakefield wanted to see unoccupied land sold in order to finance the necessary number of immigrants. Once in the colonies, the settlers should be prevented from occupying land at random. Their dispersion should be controlled.

In the 1830's private colonising companies were more active than the government in fostering practical schemes for emigration. Wakefield's ideas, therefore, were given substance in the work of the South Australia Company and the New Zealand Company. In the first year of Victoria's reign the South Australian venture was struggling to survive. Despite Wakefield's instructions it proved impossible to direct settlement minutely, and the British government did not always cooperate

A deterrent to free emigration. Convicts plundering a settler's homestead.

Edward Gibbon Wakefield. His theories of systematic colonisation were given imperfect expression in South Australia and New Zealand.

over the crucial question of land prices. Wakefield, indeed, resigned in despair from the South Australia Company. But the settlement weathered its early crises and remained. In both South Australia and New Zealand, Wakefield's imprint on early colonisation was distinctive and provided a substantial justification for his theories.

By the early 1840's British emigration to Australia averaged 15,000 a year, and in 1841 achieved the remarkable figure of 33,000. This was still small scale when compared with the intake of the United States, but it at least seemed to guarantee that the new colonies would remain British in character. In 1842 the population of New South Wales numbered 160,000, and by 1859 there were strongly established settlements not only in New South Wales but also in its now independent daughter states of Victoria and Tasmania. Western Australia had yet to find its feet and the Northern Territory was an uncharted wilderness.

Settlement had been boosted dramatically by the great Australian gold rush of the early 1850's. Beginning in 1851 with a strike near Bathurst in New South Wales, the diggings eventually centred on the rich and extensive goldfields stretching from Ballarat to Bendigo in Victoria. The feverish excitement and speculation

35

engendered by these discoveries can only be compared to the Californian gold rush of 1849 or the Rand gold strike of 1886. Within Australia itself business was disturbed, and labour (always scarce) became scarcer still. In fact, so great a dislocation of Australian society was threatened that the *Sydney Morning Herald* prophesied 'calamities far more terrible than earthquakes or pestilence'.

At first the rush was only from other parts of Australia. But as the news spread to Europe, boatloads of fortune hunters made for Victoria. In September 1852 19,000 people landed at Melbourne, and the total of immigrants in that same year reached 95,000 (a sevenfold increase) of whom less than 9,000 went to New South Wales. Only a handful of these hopefuls made anything like a fortune from the goldfields, and many of those who did succeed owed their prosperity to secondary activities such as land speculation or the provision of food and liquor. Prices rose sky-high and wages trebled. Remarkably, very few of the 'diggers' were foreign, the overwhelming majority being from Britain.

On the goldfields, tension grew over the collection of licence fees by the police. Licences cost £1 a month. The unsuccessful majority strove to avoid payment. The police, frequently corrupt and heavy-handed, were urged by the colonial government to stop evasion.

The hazards of emigration. Shipboard conditions were usually spartan, and the elements uncertain.

Australian diggers, and dog, at home.

Between October and December 1854 a lengthy and murky dispute between miners, the law, and the police led to the Eureka affair. This incident occurred when police and soldiers attacked and destroyed a stockade erected by dissatisfied miners at Eureka. Twenty-two lives were lost (seventeen of which were miners') and 120 were arrested. The miners' leaders were subsequently acquitted of high treason.

The Eureka episode, though potent in folklore, had little in common with Chartist agitation or the Paris Commune. A reasonable protest had degenerated into riot and disorder. The objects of the protest were, however, gained. Monthly licences were scrapped and an annual fee of only £1 introduced. Efforts were made to moderate police brutality, and local courts were set up on the goldfields to dispense justice speedily. The bloodiest battle between whites on Australian soil was over. It was more in the tradition of Australian trade unionism than of socialist revolution, but it illustrated the rough and ready democratic impulses of a pioneer society.

The early Australian settlements faced problems more endemic than those created by the gold rush. Indeed the gold fever at least helped one of these problems, that of attracting sufficient immigration. But ironically the migrants of the 1840's and 50's, many of them benefitting from assisted passages, aroused hostility among the established colonists. There were frequent complaints that many of the migrants selected and subsidised by the English commissioners for emigration were unsuitable, both in their skills and in their characters. This critical reaction doubtless owed a great deal to the susceptibilities of a society based so firmly on the transportation of convicts.

Another reason lay in the urban overcrowding of New South Wales and Victoria. The slums of Sydney and Melbourne, badly drained and ventilated, rivalled the worst to be found in the old country. Countless immigrants clogged the shanty towns despite the

availability of land. By the 1850's, therefore, Australia was predominantly an urban society with small townships clinging to the edge of an uninhabited continent. Lack of capital for railway development certainly inhibited penetration of the hinterland. By 1859 less than 200 miles of railway were open, and those chiefly in Victoria. Even when labourers journeyed into the interior they often found work difficult to obtain, and such work as existed was frequently seasonal – sheepshearing and the like. The comparative failure to develop rural Australia is partly explained by these circumstances.

The indigenous peoples of Australia, on the other hand, presented the Europeans with few problems. Although naturally objecting to the settlers' occupation of their hunting grounds and land, the aborigines were no match for their adversaries. What the musket and poisoned meat failed to accomplish was completed by the diseases brought by white men. Ugly massacres of blacks hardly raised a murmur of official protest. Even when missionary endeavour succeeded in establishing 'reserves', the aborigines seemed unable to adapt to their new conditions. In a few years the original 2,000 Tasmanian blacks resettled on Flinders Island had dwindled to forty-seven, and the last male died in 1869. Relying on comfortable theories of racial superiority, there were few whites to mourn the disintegration of aborigine society.

It has been estimated that at the end of the eighteenth century there were around 300,000 blackmen in Australia. By the 1860's their numbers had been reduced to tens of thousands. Although the surviving full-blooded and half-breed aborigines were able to find some sort of place in the new Australia, it was only by undertaking the most menial of tasks and entertaining the humblest of aspirations. What is more, all this occurred with the tacit approval of the authorities. There are few more disreputable chapters in the history of colonisation.

The squatters were a more serious preoccupation for the colonial government. As the Australian interior was opened up so sheepmen moved in and occupied land that did not belong to them. The crown was powerless to prevent this process. For a small outlay of capital a

Australian aborigines, with tribal scars and boomerangs, pose for the camera.

Bushranger Ned Kelly photographed the day before he was hanged at Melbourne Jail in 1880. The Kelly gang enjoyed a reign of terror of nearly two years, despite the offer of heavy rewards for their capture.

V. R.

£8000 REWARD

ROBBERY and MURDER.

WHEREAS EDWARD KELLY, DANIEL KELLY, STEPHEN HART and JOSEPH BYRNE have been declared OUTLAWS in the Colony of Victoria, and whereas warrants have been issued charging the aforesaid men with the WILFUL MURDER of MICHAEL SCANLON, Police Constable of the Colony of VICTORIA, and whereas the above-named offenders are STILL at LARGE, and have recently committed divers felonies in the Colony of NEW SOUTH WALES; Now, therefore, I, SIR HERCULES GEORGE ROBERT ROBINSON, the GOVERNOR, do, by this, my proclamation issued with the advice of the Executive Council, hereby notify that a REWARD of £4,000 will be paid, three-fourths by the Government of NEW SOUTH WALES, and one fourth by certain Banks trading in the Colony, for the apprehension of the above-named Four Offenders, or a reward of £1000 for the apprehension of any one of them; and that, in ADDITION to the above reward, a similar REWARD of £4000 has been offered by the Government of VICTORIA, and I further notify that the said REWARD will be equitably apportioned between any persons giving information which shall lead to the apprehension of the offenders and any members of the police force or other persons who may actually effect such apprehension or assist thereat.

(Signed) HENRY PARKES,
Colonial Secretary, New South Wales.

(Signed) BRYAN O'LOGHLEN,
Attorney General, Victoria.

Dated 15th February, 1879.

man could buy a flock and earn handsome profits. Wool was eagerly bought in England, and the 175,000 pounds of Australian wool sent to the mother country in 1821 had grown to 39,000,000 pounds in 1850 and comprised half the English wool imports. With such a market the squatters defied the Imperial authorities and simply appropriated the large tracts of land needed for their sheepruns.

The squatters' life was often hard. Without security of tenure there was little incentive to build sturdy homesteads. Frequently the sheepmen lived in rough huts, ate simply, and were prey to flies and mosquitoes. Labour was difficult to find and in the early days employers depended heavily on convicts. Good shepherds were rarer than gold and subsequently costly. The squatters' livelihood, moreover, could be destroyed as easily as his fortune could be made. Drought, foot rot, falling prices or eviction could bring the sheepmen crashing down in financial ruin.

In the early years of Victoria's reign the squatters were engaged in a bitter conflict with the colonial government over the price of land. The government asked for £1 an acre, which the sheepmen justifiably considered exorbitant. Substantial agitation began in England on their behalf. The textile industry feared for its supplies, the public wanted woollen goods to remain low priced. The agitators won. By 1847 the squatters were able to obtain leases for their land at a rent of £2 10s. per thousand head of sheep. The land was theirs until somebody could pay £1 an acre, and even then they had the right of pre-emption.

The squatters were safe. Their shacks were replaced by more stately dwelling places; better communications were established; the population grew and became more ordered. But although a 'squattocracy' had emerged, it by no means mirrored the English country gentry – still overwhelmingly Anglican and Tory. There were too many Catholics, radicals, Irishmen and dissenters in the Australian melting pot for that. The traditional antagonism of squatter and colonial government meant that the wealthy did not automatically associate with authority.

Not that the wealthy had any sympathy for outlaws. The bushranger was a peculiarly Australian phenomenon. A widely dispersed population and poor communications encouraged these horse-thieves and bandits. The mail, and large sums of money en route to banks were favourite targets. The most famous of the bush-rangers became enshrined in Australian folklore: Frank Gardiner, Ben Hall, Captain Thunderbolt and the Kelly gang. The task of the authorities was complicated by widespread public sympathy for the bush-rangers, whose attacks on the law and property were not unwelcome to the 'have-nots' of a pioneer society. The coming of the telegraph and the railroad ended these exploits, although the Kellys were not finally hunted down until 1880.

Constitutional advance in Australia came in the wake of similar progress in Canada. The movement towards responsible government was also stimulated by the ending of transportation and the population growth engendered by the great gold rush. By 1856 New South Wales, Victoria, Van Dieman's Land (now renamed Tasmania) and South Australia were governed by ministries responsible to elected assemblies. When in 1859 northern New South Wales became the colony of Queensland it enjoyed similar privileges. Western Australia, somewhat isolated from the eastern colonies and still taking convicts, lagged behind. In 1867 transportation ceased there as well, and in 1870 a measure of responsible government was granted.

By the mid-Victorian era, therefore, the Australian colonies were firmly established in the practice of internal self-government. They also seemed to offer unlimited opportunities for growth and development. Although subject to fluctuations, the export of Australian wool, meat and minerals promised a healthy economic future. The recent population rush had filled some, at least, of the yawning space of an empty continent. Moreover the citizens of the colonies presented a racial and cultural homogeneity to be found nowhere else in the settlement colonies. At no stage in the nineteenth century did the British percentage of the population fall below ninety-seven per cent. Although this, together with military isolation, guaranteed that on most major issues the Australian colonies would stick close to the heels of the British government, it also

The first Responsible Government of New South Wales, 1856.

meant that they had little in common with other imperial territories grappling with the complexities of race relations. The Australian experience was therefore unique and, within the broader context of the Empire, somewhat misleading.

Such niceties, however, were not the concern of immigrants and investors. Who was to know what riches would be yielded up as explorers, settlers and railroad gangs penetrated the continental void? There was, apparently, room for all. For miner, sheepman and cattle-owner the prospects seemed ripe. There was indeed some justification for the brash and confident assumption that what America had done, Australia would also do.

NEW ZEALAND   In 1836 Edward Gibbon Wakefield gave evidence before a House of Commons Select Committee on the disposal of colonial lands. Although hitherto primarily concerned with the efficient settlement of Australia, Wakefield took the opportunity to extol 'the fittest country in the world for colonisation ... the most beautiful country, with the finest climate and the most productive soil; I mean New Zealand'.

New Zealand's previous reputation had not been so benign. The Maoris were a proud and warlike people jealous of their land. European traders or sailors who outraged their customs or threatened their wellbeing usually got short shrift in return. Not that the Maori people before 1840 had much experience of the best of European manhood. The whalers, traders, and escaped convicts who battened on the North Island were a rough bunch and the growing influence of the missionaries after 1823 did little enough to soften their impact.

The British government steered clear of annexation

Title-page from an illustrated book on the Maoris, 1847. The chieftain lying on the ground bears tribal tattoos, and wears the feathers of the sacred Huia bird.

for as long as possible. Although British warships periodically visited New Zealand, it was not until 1832 that a Resident was appointed. Even then the Resident had no effective means of maintaining order, and in the circumstances 'moral suasion' was a poor substitute for a detachment of marines. Nonetheless it seemed likely that New Zealand would eventually fall within the sphere of British influence. Wakefield in fact believed that 'We are ∴.. going to colonise New Zealand . . . though we be doing it in the most slovenly and scrambling and disgraceful manner.'

It was left to Wakefield's New Zealand Company to bring some order to the scrambling. Formed in 1839 the Company faithfully reflected Wakefield's convictions that new colonies should consist of a cross section of British society. Between 1840 and 1850 the Company and its offshoots established six colonies: on either side of the strategically important Cook Strait (Wellington, Wanganui, and Nelson), and also further south at Christchurch. The activities of the New Zealand Company were probably decisive in pushing the British government into formally annexing the two islands. It is remarkable, however, that no action was taken until the first of the settlers' ships was on the high seas.

For some time the situation in New Zealand remained

The New Zealand Company settlers at Wellington in 1840. Maori longboats greet the settler ships.

tangled and uncertain. The new colonies were isolated
not only from the outer world but also from each other.
The great mountain ranges of both North and South
Island rose close to the coastline and, together with
dense rain forest, were insuperable barriers to the early
pioneers. For ten years or so the settler communities
struggled to attain economic self-sufficiency, and it was
only after this period that the lush pasture lands were
cleared and exploited for the rich sheep and dairy
farming which they offered.

There was also the problem of the Maoris, the *de facto*
owners of much of the most desirable land and for
some time in a distinct numerical superiority over the
settlers. Unlike the Australian blackfellows the Maoris
could not easily be swept aside. Recognising this fact,
the British government negotiated the 1840 Treaty
of Waitangi. Under this agreement, signed by about a
hundred chiefs, the Maoris transferred their sovereignty
to the Queen while being confirmed in their ownership
of the land. At the same time, the Treaty gave the
British government the right to purchase such land as
the chiefs might agree to sell.

The Waitangi Treaty, apparently so straightforward,
was fraught with complications. To begin with, under
customary Maori law the land belonged to the tribe
not to any individual. In addition, the agreement ran
counter to the policy of the New Zealand Company
which had already purchased land and resold it to the
incoming settlers. On both these counts many immigrants did not legally own the land they had paid for.
Over and above these considerations there loomed the
inescapable clash of European and Maori interests.
How could such a treaty contain the land-hungry
settlers indefinitely?

Both the New Zealand Company and the colonists
sought to upset the Waitangi Treaty. The Company
raised legal points, appealed to London, and tried to
avoid complying with the terms of the agreement. The
settlers pushed on regardless of legal niceties, and in
1843 serious fighting broke out with the Maoris. By
1847 the energetic efforts of the new Governor, Sir
George Grey, had brought some respite. The rebellion
was suppressed, and the Company and the government

Maori chieftains sign the Treaty of Waitangi. Their symbols are shown, right.

settled their differences. The government bought out the Company's claims to large areas of land and agreed to lend them £136,000 over the next three years. But the Company's days of independent activity were over. The government could veto the Company's decisions, and in 1850 the Company's charter was surrendered for £200,000.

Although this gave some order to the settlement of New Zealand, it by no means ended friction with the Maoris. Even if sponsored by the government, the colonists' appetite for new land grew unabated. In 1860 fresh disputes led to a prolonged war which ended in the final defeat of the Maoris in 1872. Substantial numbers of British regular troops were needed to defeat the Maori confederacy, and the fighting was characterised by some sickening slaughters of the outgunned, indigenous people.

The Second Maori War at least confirmed the inevitable. The Maoris had lost the bulk of their land in North Island to the newcomers. In South Island the native population had not been large enough to provoke a serious confrontation. From the unpromising posture of a conquered people, however, the Maoris were to be allowed to play a significant part in the future development of their country. This, though only fair, was a better fate than that allotted to the Australian aborigines.

From 1850 onwards, despite the subsequent dislocation caused by the Second Maori War, the New Zealand economy flourished. This early prosperity was based on two commodities: wool and gold. Until the introduction of refrigerated ships in the 1880's, wool remained the staple product of New Zealand agriculture. By 1851 there were nearly 250,000 sheep; in 1861 there were 2,750,000, and by 1871 the number had almost reached 10,000,000. During the same period the value of wool exports grew from £67,000 to just under £3,000,000.

While wool went almost exclusively to Britain, other agricultural produce of the 1850's (flour, live-stock, grain, potatoes, foodstuffs) found its way to Australia. This paradoxical situation was caused by the Australian gold rushes which had not only brought floods of

The Maori Wars. Maori outrages and settler retaliation lent bitterness to the struggle.

49

immigrants to Victoria and New South Wales, but had also disturbed local agriculture. New Zealand prices and wages rose, and even the Maoris were able to share in the general increase in agricultural prosperity. At the same time, the boom created more land hunger among the white settlers and brought greater pressure upon the Maoris. The latter judiciously spent a considerable proportion of their profits on firearms. Their share in economic improvement, therefore, led ironically to a sharper confrontation between them and the settlers. A confrontation, moreover, in which the Maoris were better equipped than ever before to resist encroachments on their land.

In 1857 gold was discovered in Nelson Province. In 1861 a larger strike in Otago Province (South Island) resulted in a rush which coincided with the petering out of the richer goldfields in Australia. The New Zealand gold rush exhibited the almost classical characteristics of such events. First the gold fever spread to North Island, then to the Australian colonies, then to Europe. In a matter of months Otago was elevated to a premier position among New Zealand's provinces. In one year the population trebled. Dunedin became a bonanza town, but staggered under grossly inflated prices: in the early 1860's flour could cost £52 a ton, butter 2s 6d per pound, meat 1s 1d per pound. Nearer the diggings the prices were even more outrageous.

Within a decade, however, the gold fever had burnt itself out. Dunedin suffered worse depression and unemployment than at any time since its foundation. Inevitably, only a handful of the once optimistic prospectors made their fortunes. For many the pursuit of gold brought death through exposure to the hard upland winters, or through drowning in the treacherous rivers.

The gold strikes were more significant in their secondary influences than in themselves. They attracted immigrants and capital. Between 1861 and 1870 the population of New Zealand increased from 99,021 to 248,400. In 1860 the total value of exports was £500,000; by 1863 it had leapt to £4,500,000. Although imports also rose steeply, the economy was clearly expanding vigorously.

The chief beneficiaries of these developments,

naturally enough, were the people of South Island. While North Island was being harried by the Second Maori War, the provinces of Otago and Canterbury were pushing ahead with spectacular public works, and building badly-needed roads and railways. For almost half a century, South Island surpassed its sister to the north in population and prosperity. By 1870 the boom generated by the gold rushes was over. Exports no longer outbalanced imports, and the recently acquired immigrants began to demand that the government provide them with employment. Out of these unequivocal requests grew New Zealand's desirable reputation for social welfare and the reasonable intervention of the state in economic affairs.

The growth of representative institutions in New Zealand was, at the outset, more complicated than similar developments in Australia. In 1846 New Zealand was given not only a General Assembly with an elected House, but also Provincial Councils, each with an elected chamber. These generous concessions were, however, never taken up. The main stumbling block was the position of the Maoris. The Governor, Sir George Grey, who had established cordial and constructive relations with the Maori leadership, jibbed at the prospect of their subordination to the white minority.

Matters, could not, of course, rest there. The settlers began a campaign of agitation which led to a New Zealand Constitution Act in 1852. Under the provisions

The Otago gold rush. Alluvial diggings made the fortunes of a few only. Overall, the population of South Island was boosted dramatically.

of this Act a General Assembly (consisting of two houses) and six Provincial Councils were established. The question of the Maori franchise, however, remained. Basically the British government, under the terms of the Waitangi agreement if nothing else, were committed to treating the Maoris as full citizens of the crown. Equally the settlers, still in a minority, wanted supremacy. In theory the British government stuck to its principles by making the franchise dependent upon a low property qualification. In practice, this deprived the Maoris of the vote owing to their tribal landowning customs.

When the first Parliament of New Zealand met in 1854, the triumphant settlers tried to push through to full responsible government and complete control over the disposal of crown lands. After much haggling, and the dissolving of Parliament, a responsible ministry took office in 1856. However the new Governor, Thomas Gore Browne, boldly reserved native affairs to the discretion of the crown. Rightly seeing the interests

of the two races as fundamentally antagonistic, the Governor attempted to protect the Maori people.

Such efforts were only partially successful. The settlers soon got their hands on the crown lands, although the price paid was the heavy one of the Second Maori War. Eventually the Maoris were given adult suffrage and four seats in the central legislature. The long term implication of this reform was the merging of the two races into one electoral whole. While the intention was doubtless honourable, it remained unfulfilled. In other respects, however, there seemed to be no reason why the Maoris, having been stripped of their land, should not look to a future in which they could share in their country's new prosperity and enjoy the esteem of their white fellow-citizens. In 1870 New Zealand had fair prospects and many solid virtues. If it lacked the promise of California, or the sophistication of the Old World, its qualities were by no means to be despised.

A storm-swept Barretts Hotel, Wellington, 1845. The Maoris on the shore are symbolically apart from the settler society.

3   Briton and Boer

British rule in the Cape; new and liberal policies; the Boer exodus – the Great Trek; Britain's dilemma resolved by annexation of Natal, and recognition of independence of the Orange Free State and the Transvaal; constitutional advance in the Cape, a colour-blind franchise; Sir George Grey and the movement for federation; something of the land and its white settlers.

IN THE EARLY YEARS of the Victorian age southern Africa presented British colonial policymakers with problems quite unrelated to previous experiences in North America or in the Antipodes. Towards the end of the nineteenth century these problems increased in size, complexity, and drama. At first sight, the Cape, permanently annexed by Britain in 1815, seemed unlikely to prove troublesome. There were only 27,000 Cape Dutch (or Afrikaners), and these were widely scattered by the demands of agriculture. The African tribes in close proximity to Cape Town (the Hottentots and Kaffirs) had been ruthlessly subjected to Afrikaner domination, and some indeed were slaves. Even the more formidable Bantu were kept at a distance. It seemed, therefore, that the peaceful maintenance of Cape Town as an essential base on the route to India and the Far East would be an easy matter. This, after all, was the sole object of the British annexation.

The fulfilment of this single-minded policy was extremely difficult. To begin with, the Afrikaners were not docile and obedient subjects. Composed of different nationalities (Dutch, Flemish and German, together with a strong contingent of exiled French Huguenots) the Afrikaners shared a belief in Calvinist principles and a dislike of overriding authority. They saw themselves as a racially pure elect in a black continent. Moreover, long neglected by the Netherlands' government and in any case difficult to contact, they considered

Perils of the Trek. The voortrekkers faced such physical obstacles with equanimity and endurance.

themselves their own masters. If there was anything guaranteed to unite the Afrikaner people it was an attack on their way of living, and within a few years of the annexation of the Cape the British government appeared to be launching just such an attack.

In fact, it was not quite as simple as that. The British colonial empire was governed according to certain common policies; these could not be waived to placate a few thousand Afrikaner farmers. In addition, the British administrators, missionaries and settlers who now entered the Cape had come from a social and cultural environment at odds with the rough and isolated life in the hinterland. In particular, the new adminis-tration clashed fundamentally with the Afrikaners over the treatment of the African tribes. While the British settler probably had no more wish for equality between black and white than the Afrikaner, he too was generally averse to the more brutal methods of maintaining European supremacy.

Colonial administrators were bound to consider the extent of the Imperial government's responsibility for

Simonstown naval base in the Cape. The mari-time facilities offered by the Cape had been the prime cause of the British annexation during the Napoleonic Wars.

the black majority in the Cape. It was no longer a question of leaving the problem in local hands. British missionaries, moreover, often subscribed to a less dogmatic analysis of racial differences than the Calvinist church of the Afrikaners. To many missionaries, indeed, the challenge in southern Africa was not one of subordinating the African people but of emancipating them. Given these basic attitudes, a confrontation between the British authorities and Afrikanerdom was unavoidable.

Within two decades of 1815 relations between the Afrikaners and the Imperial government had been strained to breaking point. The humanitarian standards of the administration and the liberal impulse of the evangelical missions seemed a double threat to the settled convictions of nearly two centuries. On top of this, Britain seemed determined to limit Afrikaner expansion. The reasons for this were clear enough. If the Afrikaners could be contained then it was easier to administer them. At the same time, expansion would inevitably bring clashes with the Bantu and so disturb the peace and stability of the Cape. Since the Cape's chief value to the British was as a watering and revictualling place for shipping, stability was all that was required of it.

The Afrikaners, however, saw things differently. The scourges of drought and cattle disease made the acquisition of new grazing lands imperative. So, too, did the obligation of providing farms for the numerous sons of large families. Kaffir and Bantu cattle raiders did not kindle gentle feelings in Afrikaner bosoms, and the Kaffir War of 1834–5, with its bloodshed, farm burning, and cattle slaughter, encouraged movement into more peaceful regions.

There were other resentments apart from land hunger. In 1826 the Nineteenth Ordinance of the Cape government allowed a slave to give evidence in criminal cases against his owner, and even to purchase his freedom if he could pay the appropriate price. The abolition of slavery throughout the British Empire in 1833 was an even more fundamental blow to Afrikaner susceptibilities. Although compensation was paid for the slaves in the form of government bonds these soon

fell sharply in value. When inadequate compensation was paid after the 1834–5 Kaffir War, the British government seemed tight-fisted and unsympathetic.

More important than money, however, were the social implications of emancipation. Rumours over the government's intentions accumulated. It was supposed by some that all available land was to be given to the Hottentots. Feverish imaginations foresaw government sponsored mixed marriages and the forcible imposition of Roman Catholicism. The administration's attempt to put black and white on a more equal footing before the law was said to have caused an outbreak of robbery and violence, and the misbehaviour of servants. The certainties of Afrikaner society were apparently being undermined.

Although some of the malcontents put the abolition of slavery as the prime reason for their resentment, this was not universally the case. A good many of those who eventually left the Cape owned few, or no, slaves. For them the need for new land and a determination to break out beyond the frontiers established by the British were the vital factors. Generally, though, the Afrikaners feared for their customs and were convinced that their case was never fairly represented to the Imperial authorities in London.

In the first year of Victoria's reign these resentments boiled over, and the Great Trek occurred. In one sense, the Great Trek of 1837 was merely the occasion when a greater number of Afrikaners than ever before struck off across the Orange river. There had always been movement within, and even out of, the Cape, although the pace had accelerated during the 1830's. By 1837 news had come back from those families who had already left that the land to the north was good and much of it barely inhabited. Soon several groups of voortrekkers were on the move. Led by such legendary figures as Jacobus Uys, Piet Retief, Potgeiter, and Gerrit Maritz, they went to establish a new life according to the old traditions.

As the trekkers moved into Natal and across the Orange and Vaal rivers they encountered various African peoples. While the Bamangwato or the Swazi offered little resistance, the superbly drilled and predatory Zulu and Matabele were a different proposition. Although ludicrously outnumbered, the Afrikaners were well able to take care of themselves. The stout ox-wagons could be linked into a defensive *laager*, and muskets and elephant guns decimated the ranks of the *impis*. Like Montezuma's Aztecs, many of the tribesmen had never before seen horses, and these creatures were both an object of awe and the means of voortrekker mobility. Several hundred Afrikaners, however, including Piet Retief, were slaughtered before a few decisive encounters, such as the Battle of Blood River, established European supremacy.

The Great Trek created more problems than it solved. British frontier policy was in ruins and relations with the native tribes rendered more delicate and complex than ever. Moreover, the *de facto* expansion of Afrikanerdom faced the British government with an agonising choice. Either Imperial responsibilities should be extended to the new areas opened up by the Trek, or the immigrants could simply be abandoned. Although abandonment was attractive, it would create the permanent risk of chronic conflict between Afrikaners and Bantu. There was also the possibility of foreign influence being established over the new republics. On the other hand, annexation would mean a costly and difficult administration of a people who had trekked expressly to throw off British rule.

Out of the dilemma emerged a compromise solution

Representatives of the two indigenous peoples of Cape Colony. A Hottentot horseman and his Bushman attendant.

which, although good enough in the short term, was to lead to untold difficulties. In 1843 Britain annexed Natal despite the powerful opinion of James Stephen, permanent head of the War and Colonial Office, that 'It is very ill policy to enlarge this ill-peopled and unprofitable Colony.' There was, however, some logic in the move. If Britain controlled Natal, with its Indian Ocean seaboard, then the Afrikaner republics of the Orange Free State and the Transvaal could be denied access to the sea, and thus be dependent in some measure upon British protection.

As for the two Afrikaner republics, the British government, after some hesitation, decided to placate them. It should not be supposed that this decision owed more to high-minded liberalism than to a desire for economy and non-involvement. In 1852 the Sand River Convention recognised the independence of the 15,000 Transvaalers. Two years later the Bloemfontein Convention acknowledged the sovereignty of the Orange Free State. Both treaties attempted to guarantee the security of the northern frontiers of the two republics – the chief cause of British anxieties. For their part, the British authorities were content to leave the administration of native affairs in Afrikaner hands; not that they had much choice in the matter.

The settlement was perhaps above all an exercise in co-existence. The new republics would depend ultimately on Britain for their defence and for their access to the sea. The vast bulk of their trade (especially that of the Orange Free State) would be carried on with the Cape and Natal. Britain could hope for stability and security for her maritime stations. Both sides were optimistic that a civilised dialogue would ensue. Yet co-existence was only a rationalisation of partition. While the economic and political tempo in southern Africa remained slow and steady, all might be well. A quickening of the pace, however, would place intolerable strains on British and Afrikaner alike. Divergent loyalties, traditions, and identities would then be shown in their proper light.

While the trekkers blazed their way north, the Cape of Good Hope was undergoing an equally substantial, if less dramatic, transformation. This was the establish-

ment of representative government. Since 1815 a fair number of British settlers had come to the Cape. Between 1820–1, 5,000 were landed well to the east of Cape Town in an area named Albany and with the new township of Port Elizabeth as their focal point. Although a trifling matter compared with the floods of immigrants pouring into North America, or even into New South Wales, the Albany settlement added a sizeable bloc to the European population. As in Ontario, the new settlers were used to Parliamentary government, even if they had not all previously enjoyed enfranchisement.

In 1825 the Governor of the Cape was given an advisory council to temper his hitherto complete authority. Admittedly the new council was wholly composed of officials, but in 1827 two non-officials were added. In 1834 both Legislative and Executive Councils were established. While it was true that all the members of these two councils were chosen by the Governor, the Legislative Council contained settlers who were quite capable of representing settler interests. Still, it was not representative government.

This came in 1854 when a new Parliament met in Cape Town. Both houses were elective, and thus in advance of either Australian or Canadian practice. More significant than this, however, was the fact that the Cape franchise was open to all races. The only qualification for voting was a financial one, and this was set so low that considerable numbers of Cape coloureds (people of mixed blood) as well as Bantu were

The symbol of Afrikaner mobility and independence. The trek waggon, and its occupants, opened up Natal, the Orange Free State, and the Transvaal.

Settling Natal. British
forces under Lieutenant
Farewell confronting the
Zulu chieftain, Chaka.

enfranchised. It was also technically possible for non-
Europeans to sit as members of the Cape legislature. A
very high financial qualification for candidates, however,
plus (perhaps) a certain sense of propriety, ensured that
no non-European actually took a seat during the life
of the Cape Parliament (1854–1910).

The Cape was outstanding in its open franchise. The
Transvaal and the Orange Free State maintained a
rigid racial segregation in all matters. The denial of
the vote to non-Europeans was at the bed-rock of both
republics' philosophy. When Natal was made a separate
Crown Colony, with a Legislative Council containing
a high proportion of elected members, the franchise
was theoretically similar to that of the Cape. In effect,
however, the financial qualification for voting was set
so high that few non-Europeans managed to register.

This diversity of practice, though no doubt satisfactory in local terms, carried one serious disadvantage. How could a federation of the four European-settled states in South Africa emerge when such fundamental differences existed? The Afrikaners of the Cape (a majority of the white population) were uneasy enough about the government's colour-blind franchise. Imagine, then, the feelings of the Transvaalers and Free Staters! Federation would have to reconcile these conflicts.

Surprisingly, federation was very much in the air within two decades of the Great Trek. In 1846 the Governor of the Cape was made High Commissioner for South Africa. This office provided the only shred of unity in southern Africa – and some of this was illusory. The High Commissioner was directly responsible for (say) British Kaffraria as well as claiming a disputed and insubstantial suzerainty over the Afrikaner republics. In itself, of course, the office was only as powerful as it was allowed to be. There were, however, other factors at work.

Chief of these was the tendency of the Orange Free State to look to the Cape for commercial exchanges and, in the last resort, protection. This tendency was strongly reinforced by the Transvaal's invasion of the Free State in April 1857. Led by Pretorius, the Transvaalers attempted a coup d'état to unite forcibly the Afrikaner republics. Although the invasion was rebuffed without bloodshed it stimulated disquiet in the Free State. There was, to be sure, a generally confused situation to the north of the Vaal river. In 1857 three separate republics (the South African Republic, Zoutspansberg, and Lydenburg) existed in the area later to be known as the Transvaal. They were by no means on good terms. The Transvaalers were also a good deal less advanced than the Free Staters in matters of administration and commercial orthodoxy. For instance, in 1856, while the Cape had seventeen banks and the Free State two, the Transvaal region had none whatsoever.

The Free State also recognised that in the event of a general Bantu offensive the assistance of Imperial redcoats was essential. Given these circumstances, the Cape Governorship of Sir George Grey (1854–61), provided South African federalists with a dynamic and powerful champion. Grey, fresh from his outstandingly successful administration in New Zealand, was anxious to unite not only the British colonies in southern Africa but also to bring in the Free State and even (unlikely though it seemed) the Transvaalers. Grey's hopes were torn to pieces by the Colonial Office. Especially vehement was the Under-Secretary Lord Carnarvon, although Lytton, the Secretary of State, also considered Grey a dangerous man.

The real point was that the British government had shied at the possibly expensive prospect of resuming sovereignty over the Free State, let alone any more difficult province. Grey, frequently criticised for exceeding his orders, and sometimes for compiling his own, was dismissed from the Governorship in August 1859. Although a new ministry allowed him to return to the Cape in 1860, it was only for one year and on the understanding that the federation issue was dead and buried.

It could, in any case, be argued that federation was impossible in any real sense. The European communities in southern Africa were separated by huge distances and an appalling lack of communication. Distance, historical accident, and a potent folklore were equally divisive factors. Prejudice and distrust flourished in these circumstances. All the same, the mid-1850's had looked promising for federal schemes, and it seemed to many that a more united South Africa was bound to be established eventually.

For the moment, however, there was to be no such consummation. The British colonies and the Afrikaner republics trod different paths. The Cape attained full responsible government in 1872, lagging a long way behind Canada, and the eastern colonies of Australia. Indeed, Gladstone's administration, anxious to reduce the cost of garrisoning the Empire, positively forced self-government upon the Cape which thus became theoretically responsible for its land defences. Ironically, the situation in southern Africa after 1872 forced the British government to dispatch more troops than ever before to maintain order between whites and Bantu.

Whitehall also cherished the hope that the now independent Cape, latterly enriched by the ostrich feather boom and the discovery of precious minerals, would tidy up the administrative confusion in South

Sir George Grey, Governor of Cape Colony 1854–61. A powerful advocate of South African federation, Grey was vetoed from London. He ended his remarkable career of service to the Empire by becoming Prime Minister of New Zealand.

Africa. The colony had obligingly absorbed British Kaffraria in 1865; perhaps it would now take over Basutoland, and Griqualand West where, in 1869, a shepherd boy had picked up the huge shining stone that led to the great diamond rush and the growth of Kimberley. It was anticipated that the Cape would somehow federate southern Africa from within. These hopes were by no means fulfilled. Although the Cape shouldered responsibility for Basutoland, it would not touch Griqualand West and declined to mount a campaign for a federal system. This was fair enough, for while responsible government carried certain obligations it also bestowed a larger measure of freedom.

Even before the diamond and gold discoveries in southern Africa the land was undeniably rich and, incidentally, beautiful. This was particularly true of the Cape with its magnificent mountain ranges and fertile pasture land. Architecturally, too, the Cape with its established traditions had more to offer than the pioneer territory to the north and east. Based on Dutch design, but with more spacious, airy rooms to suit the climate, the Western Province farms were solid and attractive symbols of Afrikaner settlement. Often with three or four wings, these cool, self-sufficient, white-washed buildings, with their outhouses and servants quarters had much in common with the planters' mansions of the American Deep South. They had even more in common as the focal points of an agricultural system employing large numbers of blacks and, by implication, as the fortresses of white supremacy.

If the farms of the Free State and the Transvaal lacked the aesthetic qualities of their Cape equivalents they were equally sturdy outposts of European colonisation. Hospitality was as a rule generous, and the sheltering of travellers the hallmark of a pioneer society. The bonds of family were especially strong and lengthy journeys were made regularly to visit relations. This was, after all, one way of keeping in touch and exchanging gossip. Apart from this news from the outside world travelled slowly. The literacy rate was low and few newspapers or journals available. The frontier farmer probably knew nothing of (say) Charles Dickens and perhaps little of Napoleon III. The one book he carried

Quenching thirst on trek. African servants played an important part in the migration of the Afrikaners.

with him was the bible, and his church and (if he existed) the local pastor played both a cultural and a social role. This helps to explain the extraordinary strength and political influence of the Dutch churches in South Africa.

Frontier medicine was primitive and based on ignorance, although it is only fair to add that modern medical techniques were almost impossible to dispense among such widely scattered communities. Nonetheless the homaeopathic remedies and Hottentot curatives employed were haphazard and sometimes ludicrous. Chest ailments do not readily yield to the warm skin of a freshly killed goat. But the settlers survived, perhaps mainly with the help of the large families that characterised them. Nor was there any hindrance to agricultural progress, and cattle, sheep, wheat, wine and fruit were produced in abundance and bartered for luxuries and manufactured goods.

In the towns life was a little more genteel. The first theatre in South Africa was built at Cape Town in 1800. As the nineteenth century unfolded, theatres, music halls, and organised sport developed. If the Afrikaners rejected British racial theories, they eagerly accepted the British sports of rugby football and cricket. With the establishment of schools, a flourishing local press, and improved methods of transport, towns like Cape Town, East London, Durban and Bloemfontein were able to offer facilities not greatly inferior to those of European cities.

By 1870, therefore, the European settlers in southern Africa were firmly rooted, if divided among themselves. Even the partition between British colonies and Afrikaner republics did not affect commercial and human contacts. It might also be supposed that time would soften the hard edges of political separatism and that voluntary federation would follow. By a natural evolutionary process, therefore, the richer and more populous Cape would dominate a united South Africa. It was always possible that serious trouble with the Bantu would upset this optimistic programme, or perhaps hasten it. Few, however, could have predicted that the Transvaal would prosper so spectacularly that it threatened to overshadow the Cape. But this is what was to happen when, in the words of a distinguished Afrikaner historian, catastrophe overtook the Dutch republics 'in the form of fabulous riches'.

Cape Town harbour, with Table Mountain in the background. The port was a vital link on the long run to India and the Far East.

4 India;
an Empire in the Making

The rule of the East India Company; the ever-expanding frontiers; the Afghan and Sikh Wars; Company reforms and Indian reaction; the great Mutiny of 1857; some myths and realities of the Mutiny; retribution, and 'Clemency' Canning; the aftermath of the revolt; the 1858 Government of India Act; British India.

BY 1837 BRITAIN was indisputably the paramount power in the Indian sub-continent. Beginning in the seventeenth century with small trading stations at Surat, Bombay, Madras and Calcutta, the British East India Company had subsequently extended its authority by treaty, influence and conquest. Gigantic personalities had worked out the destinies of the Company – men like Robert Clive, Warren Hastings, Richard Wellesley (brother of the Duke of Wellington) and Thomas Munro. Faced with European technological expertise, unity, and determination, a succession of powerful Indian rulers had been brought crashing from their thrones. The greatest of them all, the Mogul Emperor, remained, living out an insubstantial existence amid the ruinous decay of old Delhi.

For its part, the Honourable East India Company had assumed the powers and privileges of the fallen Moguls. As the trading activities of the Company grew less profitable in the eighteenth century, its administrative functions expanded. It drew tribute, exercised paramountcy, and came down hard on those who challenged its authority. Faced with Indian problems, the Company's servants tended to employ Indian remedies. This culminated in the accusations levelled at both Clive and Hastings for corrupt administration and personal aggrandisement.

Pitt's India Act of 1784 had given the British government an essential oversight of the Company's administration. It had also inaugurated an era of

A turbanned and bearded Sikh soldier. The military prowess of the Sikhs was utilised by the Raj after the conquest of the Punjab.

purification and reform in which Indians were theoretically guaranteed full citizenship, and equality before
the law. Considerable confusion remained, however,
regarding the exact nature of British rule. Was it best
to preserve Indian institutions and traditions or to
sweep them aside? Should docile princes be kept in
power, or reduced to the status of puppets? Would it
be possible to govern India permanently, or should
Britain be prepared at some time in the far distant
future to accept Indian self-determination?

There was also the question of the extension of the
Company's authority. By 1804 the ambitious Richard
Wellesley had crushed the Sultan of Mysore, annexed
Malabar and the Carnatic, overthrown Holkar of
Indore, and put the aged Mogul Emperor (Shah Alam)
eternally in his debt. The Company now held Bengal
and most of southern India, as well as having its powerful Residents in the courts of native princes. By 1818
the whole of central India came under British control.
Only the Punjab, Baluchistan and Sind in north-
western India were free from the Company's authority.

In the event, it was not possible to stay the Company's
hand here. The ever-expanding frontier of British India
could not be contained by directives from London.
New acquisitions made fresh acquisitions likely if not
inevitable. Despite the treaty with the Sikhs of the
Punjab it was probable that local conditions would
encourage the eventual annexation of that province.
Then Sind would follow, then Baluchistan. Perhaps
Burma would fall too. After that there was the need to
regulate relations with border states like Nepal, Afghanistan, and Persia. Ultimately it was possible to envisage
a diplomatic, and perhaps a military, clash with the
advancing influence of Russia in Central Asia.

Disquiet at alleged Russian influence in Afghanistan
precipitated a disaster for British arms. Lord Auckland
(Governor-General from 1836–42), spurred on by the
virulent Russo-phobia of Foreign Minister Palmerston,
launched an invasion of Afghanistan in 1839. Ostensibly
the action was centred on restoring the deposed King
Shah Suja in place of the Amir Dost Mahomed. In
real terms, however, Auckland hoped to throttle
suspected Russian and Persian ambitions in Afghanistan
by placing an obedient puppet on the throne. It seemed

An Amir of Sind, one of
the north-west provinces
of India brought under
the East India Company
in the 1840's.

Afghan fort guarding Kabul. The inhospitable Afghan terrain was partly responsible for the failure of both Britain and Russia to achieve the domination of Afghanistan.

likely that the Sikh leader Ranjit Singh would aid such a project. A purged and pacified Afghanistan would then provide Britain with a reliable buffer state on the north-west frontier.

Unfortunately, this analysis was grievously inaccurate. For one thing, the Russian scare was practically an illusion. Although Persia was now under Russian influence and behaving aggressively on the Afghan border, this was not the same thing as an invasion by Russia itself. The nearest Russian base was 2,000 miles from the last British outpost in India. Quite apart from supplying a large invasion force over such a distance, it was difficult to imagine the Russian armies marching unscathed through both Afghanistan and the Punjab. The Afghan Amir was, in any case, no servant of St Petersburg, and in fact preferred British influence to Russian. The maintenance of an unpopular British puppet at Kabul would also be a task requiring considerable fortitude and expense, and might pin down thousands of troops in Afghanistan. Finally, any invasion of the mountainous Afghan terrain was bound to be extremely hazardous.

Despite clear evidence that Russian and Persian influence over Dost Mahommed had been reduced to minute proportions, and in the face of the downright disapproval of the Indian Commander-in-Chief, Auckland went ahead with the invasion. Problems arose almost at once. Although Ranjit Singh had agreed to send supporting troops into Afghanistan he had insisted that Britain play the greater part. He moreover refused to allow the British invasion force through his country; thus there was the irony of the Sikhs compelling their allies to skirt the borders of the Punjab and attack the Afghans via Sind and the Bolan pass. As if this was not enough, the British troops were inadequately supplied and their commanders at loggerheads.

Kandahar, however, was occupied in April 1839, and by August Shah Suja was in Kabul. A three year fiasco ensued. Although Dost Mahommed was captured in November 1840, his supplanter, Shah Suja, was unable to rally the Afghan chiefs or consolidate his hold on the country. Meanwhile the death of Ranjit Singh threatened the Sikh alliance. Catastrophic inertia and conflict among the British command delayed an ordered withdrawal from Kabul. When at last the retreat began in January 1842 the army had to abandon a large part of its provisions and artillery and cope with hordes of camp followers as well. Harried by Afghan tribesmen, the column was massacred, one survivor only reaching the base of Jallalabad.

In February 1842 Lord Ellenborough, Auckland's successor, sent a formidable expedition to relieve the garrisons at Kandahar and Jallalabad. This was done, and the British prisoners in Kabul released into the bargain. But a complete withdrawal followed, and the striking success of the rescue operation could not disguise the overall ruin of British policy. Shah Suja had been assassinated, and Dost Mahommed restored. Thousands of troops had died and hundreds of thousands of pounds had been squandered. British influence over Afghanistan had been shattered, and, at a time when British statesmen were encouraging liberal and nationalist movements in Europe, the invasion had struck a jarring and cynical note.

Under the shadow of the Afghan disaster, however, British interests were advanced in Sind. Bullied by Auckland and forced to accept a dictated treaty, the Amirs of Sind tried to wriggle out of Britain's stranglehold. The East India Company sent the belligerent and dogged Sir Charles Napier to negotiate with them. Napier wrote, 'we have no right to seize Sind, but we

The Sikh Wars. The British conquest of the Punjab was costly and only narrowly achieved. The Sikh cavalrymen in the foreground of the illustration resemble Norman knights.

shall do so, and a very advantageous, useful, humane piece of rascality it will be'. Napier was as good as his word. He squeezed crippling concessions out of the Amirs and subsequently defeated them in a series of somewhat fortuitous battles. Despite the disapproval of the Cabinet in London, the annexation of Sind was confirmed.

The next trouble spot was the Punjab. The death of Ranjit Singh at Lahore in 1839 had plunged the province into anarchy and civil strife. In 1843 the Sikh leader Sher Singh was assassinated, and his place taken by men far less well disposed towards the East India Company. It is not difficult to see the basis of Sikh hostility. The Punjab was one of the last truly independent states of India. All round its borders the British had been nibbling away the autonomy of neighbouring provinces. Sind had been devoured ravenously. How long before the Punjab went the same way?

In December 1845 fighting broke out between the Sikhs and the British troops. The Sikhs were magnificent soldiers and also well equipped. Between December 1845 and February 1846 four ferocious and costly battles were fought. As a result the Sikhs surrendered some of their territorial claims and agreed to pay a £500,000 indemnity. Kashmir was granted to the British, who promptly sold it to a rajah for £1,000,000. Although a

Resident and a British garrison were established at Lahore, and an amicable treaty concluded in 1846, it was unlikely that matters would rest there.

In fact, the Second Sikh War began in 1848, following the departure of the popular Resident, Sir Henry Lawrence. Once more a series of bitterly contested battles resulted in a final British victory. Against almost unanimous advice the new Governor-General, Lord Dalhousie, annexed the Punjab, thus extending the frontiers of British India to Afghanistan. The brothers Henry and John Lawrence were put in charge of the province. Despite the strength of Sikh resistance to annexation, the Punjab subsequently played a stabilising role in British India. The Sikhs provided the Indian army with a large proportion of its finest soldiers, and displayed exemplary loyalty during the great Mutiny of 1857.

Lord Dalhousie,
Governor-General 1848–56.
Confident and assertive,
Dalhousie's reforms were
a prelude to the Mutiny of
1857.

British expansion did not stop here. Deteriorating relations in Burma between British merchants and the Burmese authorities led to an invasion in the spring of 1852. Rangoon fell in April, and Lower Burma was annexed. Although this was the last of Dalhousie's conquests, it was not his last annexation. The Governor-General rigorously applied the 'doctrine of lapse', which effectively prevented native princes passing on their titles to an adopted heir if they lacked a natural one. Declining to permit such adoptions, Dalhousie acquired, between 1848 and 1854, the provinces of Satara, Sambalpur, Nagpur and Jhansi.

His final and most provocative stroke was to annex the kingdom of Oudh in 1856. The 'doctrine of lapse' had nothing to do with this measure. Dalhousie's justification for his action was that the misgovernment of Oudh, and the apparent inability of its ruler to set his affairs in order, demanded intervention. In fact, the Company had no legal right to depose the King of Oudh. Its moral strictures, though doubtless genuine, were reinforced by other considerations. Chief of these was the conviction that an independent Oudh had become somewhat anachronistic amid the Company's vigorous re-ordering of things. Once under British rule, the province would offer less of a security risk, and would fit more easily into the various reforms taking place in the fields of communications and administration.

But although the annexation had this degree of logic about it, and seemed the culmination of the Company's recent policy of territorial acquisition, there were more dangerous factors to consider. Dalhousie's high-handed annexations had aroused widespread hostility. Oudh also possessed a certain significance as the last great independent Moslem state in northern India. Moreover, nearly two-thirds of the sepoys of the Bengal army came from Oudh. In 1856 they were forced to witness the humiliation of their homeland at the hands of their masters. The divided loyalties thus engendered needed careful treatment.

The Company's rule had disturbed many sections of Indian society. When princes had been roughly

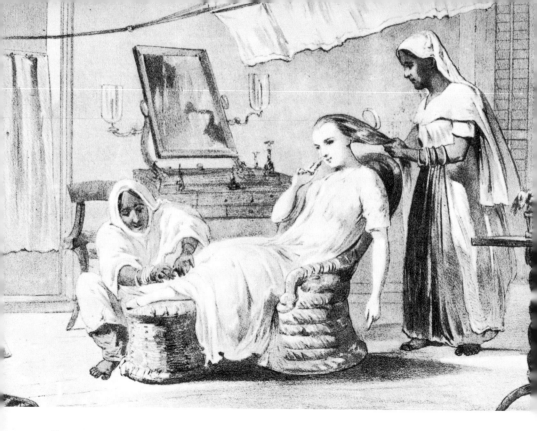

dispossessed of titles and kingdoms, groups of loyalists clung to these fallen rulers whose plight sometimes aroused wider sympathies. Also thousands of landlords unable to establish the legality of their holdings had seen their land expropriated by the British authorities.

The casual assumption of British administrators, merchants and soldiers that their civilisation was superior to Indian civilisation was a perpetual affront. Although in the early days of the Company its servants had been less aloof, the first half of the nineteenth century saw a growth in feelings of racial and cultural superiority. Whereas in the eighteenth century the British had frequently cultivated the society of Indian colleagues and merchants, this was less the case after the turn of the century. Even the pleasures of the music room and the boudoir were sacrificed. Although the common soldiery still frequented the brothels and hung around the bazaars, their superior officers took fewer Indian mistresses.

The main cause of this change was the arrival of increasing numbers of British wives. Lacking the larger duties and broader experiences of their menfolk, these

Last of the Moguls. The titular King of Delhi, proclaimed by the Mutineers in May 1857, dethroned by the British in September 1857.

76

women tended to inject an element of prejudice and narrowness into their everyday dealings with Indians. Many administrators, too, were arrogant in their judgement of Indian capabilities and contemptuous of Indian culture. The spread of evangelical Christianity, and the work of missionaries in India, also led to a feeling that the native peoples, whether Hindu or Moslem, were unenlightened and ignorant and should be shown the truth. It also happened that the utilitarian thinking which underpinned the policies of so many of the more gifted administrators demanded a radical attack on the crippling restrictions of Indian society.

There was admittedly much that was distasteful in Indian religious and cultural practice. Suttee, or widow-burning, aroused vehement hostility among the British. The clear evidence that the widows of deceased Hindu notables were frequently forced to share their husbands' funeral pyres confirmed many in their conviction that Indians were generally barbarous. The fairly common killing of unwanted girl babies, and the habit of bestowing child brides, also disturbed British

sensibilities. And what could be said of a religion which sheltered the Thugs – robbers who strangled travellers as sacrifices to the goddess Kali?

It was useless to point out that educated and progressive Indians found such customs as abhorrent as the British. By implication, all Indians were equally tainted. Secure in the growing permanence of their settlements, and convinced that their standards were correct, the British community in India applauded the Company's measures to stamp out suttee, child murder, and the Thugs. But to Indian traditionalists the Company seemed to be attacking both their religion and their cultural identity. It was curious that the basically conservative East India Company should, in the context of India, appear as the spearhead of progress and radical change.

In other spheres, too, the Company was forcing the pace. These reforms, however, sprang as much from expediency as from high principle. Centred in the fields of communications and education, the Company's efforts had been practical not idealistic. Better roads, canals, and the introduction of railways, were meant to strengthen the British hold on India as well as encouraging commerce and helping to fight famine. Similarly, educational innovations were chiefly aimed at producing adequately educated Indians for the Company's service, not at creating a westernised élite which might one day challenge British supremacy.

This process accelerated under Dalhousie's Governor-Generalship (1848–56). Confident, determined, and imaginative, Dalhousie epitomised both the vigour of British administration and some of its more ruthless qualities. In 1856 he arrived back in England amid a chorus of praise and received a pension of £5,000 a year from a grateful Company. But he had left various elements in India more restless and disturbed than at any time within the previous hundred years. Less than a year after his return the edifice of British rule in India was threatened with ruin and destruction.

The Indian Mutiny of 1857 was not simply a mutiny. Nor was it a fully-fledged nationalist revolt. Although it began when sepoys of the Bengal army mutinied at Meerut, and subsequently assumed some of the

Sepoys of the Army of Bengal before the Mutiny. Troops like these had played a conspicuous part in the extension of Company rule in India.

British soldiers of the East India Company. The Company's troops included motley and heavy-handed elements.

characteristics of a nationalist movement, the various rebel leaders had no coherent common plan. The rising was, in fact, an attempt by conservative elements to restore those pieces of the past which they cherished most, and to preserve the ancient fabric of Indian civilisation against the radical excesses and the supposed proselytising zeal of the East India Company.

The Mutiny of 1857 had its roots in deep-seated fears and resentments. There were even precedents for the outbreak. In 1806 and 1824 sepoys had mutinied, fearful that the Company was forcing them to break caste. These two revolts had been ferociously suppressed. As late as 1852 a regiment had refused service in Burma, since crossing the sea would have involved loss of caste. The Company had sensibly marched this regiment away to other duties.

In May 1857 it again seemed as if the Company was attacking the religions of its Hindu and Moslem troops. The introduction of the new Enfield rifle entailed the biting of a cartridge which was allegedly smeared with cow and pig fat. To the Hindu the cow was sacred, while to the Moslem the pig was unclean. Men of the 3rd Cavalry Regiment refused to use the new cartridge.

'Clemency' Canning, Governor-General 1856–62. During his term of office he not only put down the Mutiny, but strove to limit British retribution.

Combining coercion and tact, the Company arrested eighty-five sepoys and withdrew the offending cartridge. The next day the three regiments at Meerut mutinied, shot their officers, released their comrades and set off for Delhi.

The Mutiny took eighteen months to be put down completely. In some ways this was a remarkably long time. At the outbreak of the rising, however, there were only eleven British infantry regiments available for action, while there were over 200,000 sepoys in the Company's service. Consequently several crucial strategic points were without European troops. These included Allahabad, at the meeting point of the Ganges and the Jumna, and containing a large arsenal, and Delhi, also an important base. Lucknow and Meerut had very few British troops. The mutineers were therefore able to take these towns with ease and seize the arms and munitions.

Despite these early setbacks, the Company had much to be thankful for. The new Governor-General Lord Canning (1856–62) was able to send troops returning from Persia straight to Calcutta, and intercepted others bound for China. Of the Company's three armies, those of Bombay and Madras remained completely loyal, and only a quarter of the sepoys in the army of Bengal joined the revolt. The Indian princes gave unswerving support to the British, with the exception of the dispossessed rani of Jhansi and the Nana Sahib whose aspirations had suffered under the 'doctrine of lapse'. Recently conquered territories like the Punjab remained quiet, and border states such as Afghanistan and Nepal offered no assistance to the rebels. Indeed Gurkhas recruited in Nepal played a considerable part in suppressing the Mutiny.

No foreign power threatened to intervene, although it is difficult to see how any practical intervention would have been possible. The mutineers themselves seem to have lacked coherent leadership or any common plan. Frequently bands of them roamed the countryside looting. This may partly explain why the Indian peasantry, whose main causes were peace and subsistence, failed to join the rebels. Few Moslems lent support. Even though the Company's authority lapsed for a time in Delhi, Oudh, north-central India, and some of Bengal, two-thirds of the country remained absolutely passive. In real terms, British supremacy was not seriously threatened. It is, moreover, tempting to explain the stubbornness of sepoy resistance in the light of the retribution meted out to them; death in battle was preferable to death at the hands of the avenging British.

In comparison to contemporary campaigns (the Crimean War, for instance, or the American Civil War) the Indian Mutiny involved small numbers of men. The main problems for the British forces were those of

distance and supply. There was also the usual amount of ineptitude and rivalry among the military commanders, a situation somewhat exacerbated by the existence of two armies – that of the East India Company and that of the British government. Despite this, some extremely able, even remarkable, British generals helped put down the Mutiny: the Lawrence brothers; Havelock, in demeanour more like an evangelical bishop than the reliever of Lucknow; John Nicholson, so dominating a figure that an Indian sect had been formed to worship him; Hugh Rose, whose brilliant campaigning in the Rajput states (where he travelled fast and dressed his men in khaki rather than regimental red) owed something to his Prussian training.

Of more lasting significance, however, than the skills of individual generals were the dark and brutal episodes of the Mutiny. Contemporary British opinion was gorged on a diet of gruesome sepoy atrocities and heroic British counterstrokes. It is certainly true that several hundred British women and children were murdered in the confusion of the rising – most of them on the orders of the notorious Nana Sahib. Doubtless some English women were raped too. It was futile to point out that the expansion of British authority in India had occasioned similar bloody deeds, or that British soldiers had been responsible for countless outrages against Indian women.

British propagandists chose only to dwell on sepoy enormities. The mutineers were depicted in cartoons and prints as ravening, lustful wolves; barbaric,

Fire, sword and rapine. A propagandist print of the Mutiny entitled 'English Homes in India, 1857'.

Massacre at Delhi, 1857.
The English children
tossed on sepoy bayonets
have much in common
with the Belgian infants
allegedly slaughtered by
the Germans in 1914.

revengeful, hardly human. Where previously the sepoys
had been considered as the brave mercenaries of the
Company, they were now portrayed as tearing with
reeking hands at the pure bosoms of English woman-
hood, or tossing rosy English babies upon their bayonets
for sport. The racist undercurrents stirred up by these
images were to have long-lasting effects. Although
Queen Victoria strongly disapproved of the term
'nigger' to describe her Indian subjects, it seemed to
many that the sepoys had behaved like savages just out
of the jungle.

British retribution was, in the event, terrible. It is,
of course, easy to understand the emotions of soldiers
like the young Garnett Wolseley on discovering the

dismembered bodies of women and children at Delhi: 'Had any Christian bishop visited that scene of butchery when I saw it, I verily believe that he would have buckled on his sword'. Nonetheless, British troops went to unpalatable lengths to revenge their nation. Moslems were sewn into pig skins prior to hanging, a fate so horrible for a devout follower of Islam as to defy description. At Delhi, captured sepoys were made to lick up from the floor the congealed blood of their victims. Those rebels who were blown into fragments of flesh and bone from the mouths of cannon, or summarily hanged, were comparatively fortunate.

This whirlwind of revenge swept through Lucknow, Cawnpore, Delhi and Gwalior. In the circumstances, the Governor-General Lord Canning was hard pressed to earn his nickname of 'Clemency' Canning. It is evident, however, that his restraining hand reduced indiscriminate retribution. If a more oppressive Governor had held office, a far more discreditable chapter would have been written. But Canning had got his priorities right. The vindictiveness of the suppression of the Mutiny had encouraged resistance to the last man, and had cost more British lives than had been necessary.

Retribution. Bones and skulls litter a courtyard at Lucknow, where two thousand sepoys were bayonetted by the relieving army.

Hanged mutineers. In some instances, Moslem sepoys were hanged in pig-skins as a special punishment.

Since the British administration had got to cope with the aftermath of the revolt, it could best do so if Anglo-Indian relations were damaged as little as possible.

Clemency did not, however, soften the bitter hatred left by the Mutiny. Deep-seated prejudices which had already been much in evidence before 1857 were confirmed and strengthened. The gulf which had already opened between the two races widened to almost unbridgeable proportions. Distrust was heightened. How could the British officer, merchant, or even administrator, see Indians in the same light ever again? In a matter of moments, apparently steadfast soldiers and loyal servants had been transformed into murderous fiends. East was East and West was West and *never* the twain could meet, it seemed. Subsequently, among the casualties of the Mutiny were some of the more liberal assumptions concerning Indian progress and political development.

These trends were reflected in the literature of the post-Mutiny period. A considerable number of imaginative writers who dealt with India chose to stereotype Indians as treacherous, lazy, and unreliable. Indian culture was neglected, and where it was not neglected scorned. The passive and contemplative qualities of Hinduism were dismissed as unmanly in comparison with the flexing muscles of public school Christianity. There were, of course, *some* good Indians, but these were found chiefly among pacific villagers or among the keen-eyed tribesmen of the north-west frontier.

The Indians, too, recoiled from the horrors of the Mutiny. The growing westernised élite, educated according to English principles and as likely to read Tom Paine as Jane Austen, continued to serve the administration at a secondary level. But, no matter how impeccable their English or how genuine their appreciation of Shakespeare, they remained Indians, ruled, in their own land, by aliens. A more militant attitude would grow out of their predicament. This was all the more likely when British theory and practice were so often at odds. Since 1853, for example, Indians had been able to compete by examination for places in the Indian Civil Service. But the difficulties of travelling to England for the competition were insuperable unless one was very rich, and, if a Hindu, prepared to lose caste by crossing the seas. Thus between 1853 and 1871 only one Indian managed to enter his country's civil service.

Orthodox Hinduism was also revived by the Mutiny. Whereas before 1857 reformist elements had been in the ascendant, the subsequent reaction exalted the more obscure and traditionalist qualities of Hinduism as a protection against the inroads of British ideas and influence. Yet another bastion of conservatism was reinforced by the Mutiny. The Indian princes had displayed almost unanimous loyalty during the rising. They now reaped their reward. The British administration clearly regarded them as stalwart supporters of the régime. Accordingly the princely states were safe from encroachment as long as they accepted British overlordship. Another bonus for the princes lay in the caution exercised by Britain over possible reforms. Fearful to set in motion an Indian reaction similar to that before 1857, the government avoided drastic political and social change.

The more formal results of the Mutiny contained a good deal that was insubstantial. Under the 1858

Shattered gateway opposite the Residency, Lucknow.

Mutineers about to be blown from field pieces at Peshawur.

Government of India Act the power of the East India Company was swept away and assumed by the crown. But for all practical purposes the British government had been the masters of India since 1813. Now, however, theory had been brought into line with practice. The Company continued as a trading concern, but it was like a great creature worn out by the years and hollow inside. The Governor-General was given the title of Viceroy by Royal Proclamation, but carried out the same duties. In order to sharpen its authority in London, the government established a Secretary of State for India and a council of fifteen to advise him.

The existence of a Secretary for India responsible to Parliament and advised by the India Council was not without its problems. At the beginning, the India Council consisted of ex-servants of the Company and tended to be conservative. The Secretary of State could, if he wished, ignore its feelings and base his authority on Parliament. Here, too, parliamentary supervision could only be effective if members made it so. Since Indian affairs were remote from the interests of most M.P.'s, the Secretary of State could often carry on as he and the Cabinet thought fit. But even given a masterful Secretary of State and a compliant Parliament, there was still the matter of supervising and, if necessary, controlling the Viceroy.

Distance rendered this latter task a difficult one. It took six months for a letter to pass between Calcutta and London. By the time the Viceroy had informed the British government of a crisis, it was frequently over. Even if given clear instructions from Whitehall, a determined Viceroy could waste literally years in prevarication. He could, of course, be recalled, but as 'the man on the spot' he had enormous power and was difficult to unseat. In 1870, however, this state of affairs was radically altered by the opening of a telegraph link between India and Britain. Direct communication with the Viceroys gave them much less chance to wriggle, although a good deal of wriggling continued to take place.

In India itself there was some attempt to broaden the framework of government. The Central Legislative Council was expanded in 1861 by the addition of several non-official members, of whom two were Indians. This was, however, an almost worthless reform. The Legislative Council had hardly any legislative functions, and no power at all over the Viceroy's Executive Council. The two Indian non-officials were safe loyalists, not seditious politicians. The Viceroy's Council, moreover, was untrammeled by any such democratic forms, and it was the Viceroy's Council that ruled India. One other administrative development is worthy of note. This was the restoration of legislative functions to the councils of Bombay and Madras, and the establishment of legislative councils for Bengal, the Punjab and the north-west provinces. But here again the power was more illusory than real, though the councils could conceivably be utilised as vehicles of democratic experiment.

The army, naturally, was reconstructed after the Mutiny. All its troops were placed under the crown. More significant than this was the increase in the proportion of British soldiers, and the refusal to let Indian troops handle artillery. Since, however, Indian soldiers continued to outnumber British soldiers by two to one, an attempt was made to recruit reliable men. Subsequently the Indian army came to rely heavily on Sikhs, Gurkhas, and the frontier tribes; the numbers of orthodox Hindus and Moslems declined. There was even talk at Viceregal level of a massive recruitment in Burma, Ceylon, and Borneo. Africans also were considered, but the authorities feared hostile Indian reactions. Thus reformed, the Indian army was a readily available, reliable, and loyal instrument of Imperial policy. As the traditionalist Viceroy Lord Lawrence (1863–9) put it, 'We conquered India by force of arms and in like manner we must hold it'. It was ironical all the same that Indians continued to play the main part in holding India.

A new legal code was introduced in two Acts of 1859 and 1861. The latter Act confirmed the supremacy of the High Courts and extended them on a nation-wide scale. In this way, a more unifying legal framework was erected. By 1868 the Indian government had

Dustman: 'I don't quite like the looks o' this 'ere Hingia bisnis, Tommy!' Sweep: 'No; but it's just wot yer might expeck from sich a parcel o' dirty black hignorant scoundrels as them.'

also come to accept its responsibilities for alleviating the disasters of famine. This was, for the times, an unusually progressive declaration of a welfare policy. With the slow but appreciable expansion of education, the government could claim some credit for concerning itself with Indian interests. Generally speaking, however, such reforms took place within a specifically English context. Progress, when it occurred, was only possible to the strains of 'God Save the Queen'.

Foreign policy after the Mutiny was somewhat restrained. 'Clemency' Canning showed no strong desire to acquire more territory, and his successor Lord Elgin believed that the Indian government should meddle as little as possible in Afghan affairs. Although in 1863 there was some disturbance on the Afghan frontier, the death of the Amir Dost Mahommed in the same year led to half a decade of internal confusion in Afghanistan. This meant that for all practical purposes the Indian government could ignore Afghanistan. It was no longer necessary either to bribe the Amir regularly or overawe him with force of arms. When in

The men who ruled India. The Governor-General, Lord Lawrence (centre, right), and his Executive Council.

1868 a new Amir, Sher Ali, had emerged, the Viceroy, Lord Lawrence, met him amicably and made him a gift of twelve lakhs of rupees and 6,000 muskets.

As regards Russian expansion in central Asia, Lawrence took the sensible course of doubting the real dangers to India and expressing hopes for an Anglo-Russian agreement. Both Liberal and Conservative governments in the 1860's tended to agree with this approach, and awaited the opportunity for an understanding with Russia. It was, however, always likely that strident demands for a 'Forward' policy on the north-west frontier would be revived. But for the time being India seemed to be guaranteed peace and security.

By 1870, therefore, British India stood pacified and, to some extent, reformed. Economic progress was made, and there were improvements in the fields of communication, education, and agricultural methods. Thus, overall, India became more *British*. The numbers of British officials and non-officials increased markedly, and Anglo-Indian society became more self-contained and self-confident as a result. There was even an attempt to attract European settlers.

The self-assurance of the British community was, however, often near to arrogance. And while it was convenient to despise Indians, there was also the uncomfortable feeling that one day they would entertain inconvenient political and social ambitions. Few denied that Indians could, of course, be clever; indeed, could be trained in any number of skills. But could they act like gentleman, and bear, without much reward, the crushing burdens of imperial responsibility? That was another matter. While such attitudes persisted a genuine dialogue between the two races was out of the question. By the mid-Victorian age, the white man's burden in India had become the colour of his skin.

5 Scattered Possessions

The dependent territories in 1837; limited Imperial ambitions; the West Indies in turmoil; the emancipation of the slaves, and the slump in the sugar industry; black freedmen and white planters; Governor Eyre and the repression of the 1865 Jamaica Rebellion; Crown Colony rule in the Caribbean; British interests in West Africa, Ceylon, Malaya and Borneo; conflict with China and the acquisition of Hong Kong; the building and opening of the Suez Canal.

West Indian slaves receiving news of their emancipation, 1833. Emancipation was to lead to grave political, social and economic dislocation. Note the sugar mill in the background.

Imperial outpost. Women on the shore of the lonely Atlantic island of Tristan da Cunha.

APART FROM INDIA and the colonies of white settlement, the rest of the Empire in 1837 was of a motley character. The West Indian colonies were remnants of the First Empire – and somewhat tattered remnants at that. On the west coast of Africa there was the Crown Colony of Sierra Leone, and various trading stations on the Gold Coast. Whereas some of the latter had previously dealt in slaves, they now exported gold, ivory, and palm oil. Interest had also been awoken in the palm oil trade of the Niger delta. Over the east coast of Africa Britain exercised influence through the pliable Sultan of Zanzibar, but as yet held no territory.

Similar influence was wielded in the Persian Gulf and the Red Sea. A network of local rulers and British Residents were backed up by the ubiquitous Royal Navy. This was gunboat diplomacy in its most classical form. Elsewhere a string of possessions bore witness to the needs of a maritime nation and to the prime importance of safeguarding the route to India. Thus Britain had acquired St Helena, Ascension, Gibraltar, Malta, Aden, Mauritius, the Seychelles, and Tristan da Cunha as naval outposts and bases.

In Eastern waters strategic and commercial expediency had brought Ceylon, Penang, Malacca and Singapore under British rule. Singapore provided an outstanding example of brisk commercial development under the Union Jack; purchased in 1819 from the

Sultan of Johore, Singapore had grown in four years from a desolate island to a port with an annual trade of £2,500,000. It was, moreover, likely that British influence would eventually be extended not only in Malaya, but also in China.

In many ways, however, the period 1837–70 was not one of vigorous colonial expansion. One of the chief reasons lay in the break-up of the Empire's rigidly controlled mercantilist system. By the 1850's, on Britain's initiative, free trade had largely replaced protection. Colonial possessions were not therefore central to commercial policy. Trade agreements between individual parties became common practice. To this end, it was more appropriate to exert skilful diplomatic pressures than annex unprofitable territory. Dominion over untutored savages seemed less important than coastal influence and a dividend of 5% on investments.

While this commercial revolution occured, relations between the great European powers remained generally peaceful. After 1815, for example, Britain did not

West African chiefs, with top hats and umbrellas, in the British colony of Sierra Leone.

David Livingstone (1813–73). As both missionary and explorer, Livingstone did much to focus popular attention on the 'dark continent'.

West African
missionary on his rounds.

go to war with another European country until the
Crimean outbreak in 1854, and subsequently stayed at
peace until 1914. In these circumstances, there was
little opportunity for European conflicts to spill over
into military competition for colonies. In any case the
naval supremacy of Britain gave her unprecedented
authority outside Europe. If bitterly opposed by
Britain, it was difficult to imagine any practical extension of European colonialism.

The Empire aroused conflicting emotions among the
early Victorians. Given the continuing surge of commercial activity (and profits) it was tempting for
manufacturers and financiers to equate free trade, and
the loosening of colonial bonds, with an expansion of
commerce. Much official opinion, from Sir James
Stephen to Peel and Palmerston, took a pragmatic view
of the existing colonial connection and foresaw (with
no great misgivings) the emergence of Canadian and
Australasian republics. This prognosis was admittedly
tempered by a certain amount of national self-interest,
but seemed realistic all the same. Industrialists and
exporters were of the same mind. More sophisticated
still was the theorising of Cobden, who argued that
dependant colonial status in some measure degraded
both colony and mother country.

Underlying the separatist advocacies, however, was
the assumption that the severing of the imperial link
would not disturb the commercial relations of Britain
and the colonies. Just as Anglo-American trade had

97

boomed after the rebellion of the Thirteen Colonies, so it was probable that a similar pattern would follow other secessions. Some went one stage further than this and claimed, with Jeremy Bentham, that colonies had a postively harmful effect on the national economy; that they created artificial markets, were costly to maintain, and could drag Britain into unnecessary international conflicts.

But Benthamite radicals did not go so far as to press for the dissolution of the Empire. The colonies were, after all, arenas for social experiment, and had already developed some healthy democratic characteristics. In addition, the Radical Imperialists (men like Lord Durham, Wakefield, Charles Buller) were profoundly opposed to any cutting of imperial bonds. Instead, they hoped that, by judicious reform and sensible management, the colonies of white settlement could not only be induced to stay in the Empire but would become its ornament and a source of incalculable strength.

Despite these optimistic assessments, early Victorian governments were by no means convinced that a substantial extension of the Empire was worthwhile. It was one thing to make efficient use of territories already possessed, quite another to finance fresh colonial undertakings of questionable profitability. In particular it seemed folly to annex tropical colonies with large non-European populations. In the 1830's the existing colonies in this category were troublesome enough.

The British West Indies contained some of the oldest settlements in the Empire. St Kitts, Barbados, Nevis, Antigua and Monserrat were colonised in the 1620's; Jamica was conquered by Cromwell in 1656. Subsequent conquests brought a whole crop of islands, including Trinidad, under British rule. The sugar revolution of the 1640's transformed the economies of the West Indies. A huge slave population was transported across the Atlantic, often under the vilest conditions, to work on the sugar plantations. The profits from sugar rocketed, and remained high for well over a century.

This economic revolution had far-reaching effects. Riding on the tide of profitability, the West Indies took pride of place among colonial possessions. They were less difficult to control than the mainland colonies, and easier to administer than Bengal. Sugar interests were powerful in the City and extremely influential in the unreformed House of Commons. But the establishment of slavery had the effect of displacing many white settlers in the West Indies. Barbados, for example, had 40,000 whites to about 6,000 blacks in 1645; in 1685 the ratio was about 20,000 to 46,000, and by 1700 the white population had shrunk to 12,000.

Since the British West Indian islands had been endowed with similar representative institutions to the mainland colonies, this meant that power was now concentrated in the hands of a few white planters. The 'plantocracy', greatly outnumbered by their black slaves, were jealous of their privileged political status and fearful of the results of economic and social change. They were overwhelmed with such changes in the early years of the nineteenth century. By the turn of the century the bottom had been knocked out of the sugar market. In response to humanitarian pressures and economic facts, but also with an eye to political expediency, the British government prohibited the slave trade in 1807. In 1833 an Act abolishing slavery was carried through Parliament.

White planter, black servant. West Indian emancipation at first did little to alter the relationship between the 'plantocracy' and the ex-slaves.

The early years of Victoria's reign saw attempts to deal with the implications of emancipation. 512,823 slaves had been freed in the West Indies, over half of them in Jamaica. Recognising the rights of property (even human property) Parliament agreed to pay £20,000,000 in compensation. Although this was a handsome sum, the final figure paid out was only £18,669,401. Much of this, moreover, went straight to the planters' creditors in England. But initially the planters had the advantage of an apprentice system in lieu of slavery. Under this arrangement all ex-slaves over six years old were bound to work for their former masters under terms which were not much better than before emancipation. Although all apprenticeship was due to end in 1840, the immediate effect was to tie ex-slaves to their plantations and provide employers with very cheap labour.

The inadequacies of the apprenticeship system were soon revealed. Abolitionists in Britain attacked it as covert slavery. Certainly it was attended by much maladministration and abuse. Workers were paid in

Edward John Eyre.
While Governor of
Jamaica, his repression
of the 1865 Rebellion led
to his dismissal from office
and precipitated a
readjustment of Colonial
Office policy.

kind and could not easily re-sell these goods. The forty
hours to be worked per week were often spread over six
days, thus leaving negroes little time to cultivate their
own smallholdings. Conditions in workhouses were
appalling, and the punishments allowed (including
flogging) no better than on a badly-run plantation. The
system was so plainly unsatisfactory that the colonial
legislatures voluntarily scrapped it in 1838.

With the end of apprenticeship, the planters were
hard pressed to keep their negroes working on the
sugar estates. The now fully emancipated slaves drifted
off the plantations and set up as smallholders growing
coffee, food crops, or ginger. The planters had now to
contend with a chronic labour shortage, as well as the
problems of inadequate capital and fierce competition
from foreign sugar. A further shattering blow was

Britain's abandonment of sugar protection in 1854.

No colony was harder hit than Jamaica, where there were 859 sugar estates in 1804, but only 330 in 1854. In roughly the same time sugar production fell by over half, and between 1828 and 1850 Jamaica's share of the world total sugar production plunged from 15% to 2·5%. In desperation, the planters scoured the globe for labour. Workers came from Britain, Germany, even the United States. More satisfactory sources were Indian and Chinese coolies, many thousands of whom were brought across the Atlantic under indentures. Sugar, however, was no longer King; instead, he resembled a down-at-heel Pretender clutching about him the rags of his former glory.

The West Indian plantocracy took their misfortune ill. Many adopted the simple course of blaming the British government and the alleged laziness of the negroes. A fair number of the latter were certainly working leisurely, though fairly profitably, on their smallholdings, but this, after all, was what they were entitled to do. The planters were perhaps more to blame for their refusal to invest sufficiently in new plant and equipment. Despite this, a myth arose, ardently propagated by apologists like Thomas Carlyle, that the black man was ruining the West Indies by lolling around up to his ears in water melon. According to this legend, order and prosperity had been replaced by anarchy, insolvency and insolence.

The Colonial Office would probably have preferred to see the gradual substitution of white oligarchy by multi-racial democracy within the terms of the old colonial constitution. It was clear, however, that the planters were in no mood to surrender their privileges and accept political, not to speak of social, equality. If left to them, the West Indian negroes would have been whipped back on to the plantations where they belonged. As more coloured West Indians began to demand a greater share in government a crisis was always likely.

The crisis came with the Jamaica Rebellion of 1865. Engendered by the genuine grievances of the negro peasantry and by the intolerance of the plantocracy, the disturbances at least solved the problem of the immediate direction of West Indian constitutional development. Two figures dominated Jamaica in 1865. One was the Governor, Edward John Eyre; the other George William Gordon. Eyre came to the Governorship after a worthy enough career as an administrator in Australia (his adopted country), New Zealand, and then the West Indies. His record with non-European people was hitherto perfectly respectable. Indeed, in Australia he had been appointed a district Protector of the Aborigines (a thankless task), and later in Trinidad he had briefly held the post of Protector of indentured Indian immigrants. For all this, Eyre had a low opinion of non-Europeans, and in Jamaica fell speedily under the influence of intolerant and powerful planter interests. As Governor, he was obdurate, reactionary, and not particularly intelligent.

His opponent, Gordon, was of mixed blood, but the son of a wealthy white planter, and a member of the Jamaica House of Assembly. Gordon was, therefore, uniquely placed both to feel for the black peasantry and to give voice to their grievances. His tactics were those of unrestrained and, in the circumstances, courageous abuse of Eyre's methods. For his part, Eyre retaliated by removing Gordon from the magistrates' bench, and refusing point blank to listen to his representations. The Colonial Office, though well aware of Eyre's shortcomings, had little option but to support the Governor. Meanwhile Gordon indulged in a series of passionate public speeches in which he attacked alleged government corruption and the failure to administer properly various relief schemes.

In October 1865, at Morant Bay, the site of one of Gordon's hard-hitting speeches, a crowd of negroes broke into a court house and rescued one of their fellows on trial there. They subsequently resisted arrest, and finally killed the twenty-two men of a volunteer force sent against them. At this point, Eyre lost his head. With cool handling, the whole affair might have been easily contained. But fed on the lurid prospects of black revolution, and tempted by the chance to strike at Gordon, Eyre acted with intemperance and ferocity. All local forces were mobilised, reinforcements summoned from as far away as Canada and the Bahamas, and martial law proclaimed.

One of the most discreditable episodes in British

Start of the 1865 Jamaica Rebellion. Attack on the court-house at Morant Bay.

colonial history ensued. The military shot, hanged, and flogged on the slightest provocation. Summary executions were frequent, house-burning commonplace. Evidence later submitted to a Royal Commission revealed horrifying details:

Having flogged nine men and burnt three negro houses, we then had a court-martial on the prisoners .... Several were flogged without court-martial on a simple examination. One man ... got fifty lashes; one man got one hundred.

... shot nine and hung three; made rebels hang each other; effect on the living terrific.

In all, 439 negroes died, of whom 354 were executed after court-martial. Many more were flogged barbarously; over 1,000 houses were burnt. Gordon was arrested in Kingston, where martial law had not been proclaimed, taken to Morant Bay and hanged within a few hours of his court-martial.

The British government reacted speedily to these outrages. Eyre was suspended, and a Royal Commission appointed. The Commission praised Eyre for his prompt action, but condemned the excesses perpetrated under martial law. It also denied that the martyred Gordon was involved in any conspiracy. Eyre was recalled in disgrace, although he remained a hero to such prejudiced observers as the hero-worshipping Carlyle. Brought to trial in England, the dismissed Governor's supporters launched an Eyre Defence Aid Fund; their opponents organised the Jamaica Committee. Eyre was, however, acquitted of his misdemeanors and lived to receive a state pension from Disraeli's government in 1874.

In broader perspective, the Jamaica rebellion provided the British government with the opportunity to sweep away anachronistic colonial constitutions in the West Indies. Crown Colony rule was established in Jamaica and a host of smaller islands. Although Barbados, Bermuda, the Bahamas, and British Guiana kept their ancient institutions, these were now the exceptions in the Caribbean. Crown Colony rule was fundamentally autocratic in the mid-nineteenth century; but at least it placed power in the hands of a supposedly impartial Colonial Office. At worst, it denied overlordship to an insular white minority while not handing over government to an uninstructed

coloured majority. At best, it provided the basis from which to begin the long haul towards responsible self-government.

Elsewhere the British government was, with some reluctance, assuming direct control over a variety of tropical territories. In 1843 it took over those Gold Coast settlements hitherto entrusted to a committee of merchants. In 1850 Britain bought out Denmark's Gold Coast stations, and in 1871 carried out a similar transaction with the Netherlands. Lagos became a Crown Colony in 1861. By these means Britain had established herself as the paramount power on the West African coast by 1870. And this was in the face of the famous Commons' Committee recommendation of 1865 that (with the possible exception of Sierra Leone) all Britain's West African possessions should be surrendered.

No such surrender took place however. Nor did it in the Crown Colony of Ceylon. Here, at the tip of autocratically ruled India, was a British possession which was destined to undergo some remarkable constitutional experiments. This progress was all the more remarkable because it lacked the sustained bitterness of similar developments in India. Ceylon was not without racial problems either, for its population was composed of Sinhalese, Tamils, Moslems (descended from Arabic stock), and the products of interbreeding between the Portuguese, the Dutch, and Ceylonese women. Perhaps, however, the key to Ceylon's relatively smooth constitutional progress lay in the simple fact that, apart from the Trincomalee naval base, the British set no great store by this colony.

At any rate, as a result of a Commission in 1833, the Governor of Ceylon was given an Executive and a Legislative Council. The latter had a minority of non-official members of whom half were to be Sinhalese, Tamils or Burghers (of Dutch descent). It was true that the non-European element was small, but it was clearly capable of growth. Moreover, after 1867 the Legislative Council had control over the Ceylon budget. Given the absence of a permanent British community it seemed likely that Ceylon would become the first non-European colony to achieve responsible govern-

Ruins of the old slave-trading fortress at Christiansburg, near Accra.

ment although, in the event, the goal was a long way off.

In Malaya the British extended their authority in order to maintain their influence. The activities of pirates and unending local conflicts made it essential to protect British commercial interests. The British Straits Settlement (Penang, Malacca, and Singapore) were transferred from the Indian to the Colonial Office in 1867. Thereafter, British policy relied heavily upon treaty-making with the Malay states and upon a network of Residents in local courts. Such involvement was, however, likely to lead to more direct intervention.

Sarawak, in North Borneo, provided an eccentric exception to the more mundane methods of British

Kandyan Chiefs, Ceylon. The ancient inland kingdom of Kandy remained for some time resistant to British rule in Ceylon.

Planter's bungalow, Ceylon. Both verandah and servant gave some comfort to ex-patriate Britons managing tea-growing estates.

Sir James Brooke blowing pirates out of the water; off the coast of Borneo, 1843.

The rewards of enterprise. Sir James Brooke as hereditary Rajah of Sarawak.

colonial expansion. Here James Brooke, an ex-servant of the East India Company, gave invaluable assistance to the Sultan of Brunei in suppressing pirates. In 1846 Brooke was given Sarawak to rule under the suzerainty of the Sultan. The mid-Victorian Empire was thus adorned with a white Sultan of Sarawak, reigning as Rajah Brooke, and able to pass on his title to his descendants.

China was yet another area of British activity. Here, as elsewhere, the interests were commercial. The methods employed in defence of these interests were, however, unsavoury and in the last resort, brutal. Initially, British interest in China had centred on the East India Company's need to buy tea at Canton for re-export to other parts of the world. Unfortunately the most lucrative Indian commodity to exchange for tea was opium. The Imperial government of China banned the importation of this drug in 1800, but opium smuggling took place on a vast scale until the firm measures of Commissioner Lin in 1838.

The British government retaliated with unashamed and completely indefensible aggression. The Royal Navy efficiently routed the Imperial Chinese squadrons, and Britain proceeded to dictate a humiliating treaty to the once haughty Chinese authorites. Under the terms of the Treaty of Nanking, Britain received Hong Kong, and was allowed to trade at four other treaty ports. In all these ports, British subjects were exempt from Chinese jurisdiction and the authority of the Pekin government diminished.

With the minimum of effort Britain had acquired the maximum commercial and political benefits. Thousands of years of civilisation had been of no avail against a few frigates and a small but well-equipped expeditionary force. The front door to China was now open. Although Palmerston dismissed Hong Kong as 'a barren island with hardly a house upon it', British merchants knew better. The annexation delighted them, and fulfilled their slogan of 'Hong Kong, deep water and a free port for ever!' Other European nations now hurried to squeeze similar concessions out of the Chinese government. China's century of foreign domination and abuse had begun.

By the 1860's the British Empire seemed to be securely based on the results of settler initiative and commercial enterprise. Territorial committments were only grudgingly accepted by Westminster, while there was a positive eagerness to free the British government from the expensive burden of local colonial defence. Rather than run up the Union Jack, the Cabinet preferred to exert diplomatic pressures. If these failed there was

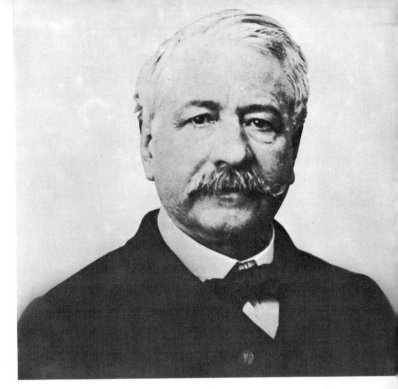

Ferdinand de Lesseps.
Founder of the Suez
Canal Company; begetter
of the Suez Canal.

The Opium Wars.
Storming ladders and
dead defenders festoon a
Chinese fort in 1860.

always the persuasive eloquence of the Royal Navy's
guns. Although fresh scraps of territory had found their
way into the dependent Empire by 1870, their acquisition had been, on the whole, a matter of fine calculation rather than indiscriminate plundering.

Mid-Victorian statesmen were in no hurry to sacrifice
this ordered and fundamentally inexpensive approach
to Empire. By 1869, however, the opening of the Suez
Canal threatened to destroy such leisurely calculations.
The short cut to the East, via Suez, sharpened international rivalry in the eastern Mediterranean and Africa,
while removing some of the significance from Britain's
possession of the Cape.

The Canal project had always been capable of
generating the most violent passions, and its construc-
tion was bedevilled with problems. The history of the
Suez route, however, was a long one. In the seventh
century BC a canal of sorts had existed between the
Nile and the Red Sea. Later the waterways silted up.
Although trade continued to flow overland, the
Portuguese discovery in 1487 of the Cape route to
India diverted commerce from the Levant and from
Marseilles. Both the Venetians and Louis XIV con-
templated cutting a new canal. France in particular

cherished a project which promised to restore the old Mediterranean prosperities and damage the new Atlantic powers of Britain and the Netherlands. In 1799 Bonaparte's engineers got as far as surveying possible routes, although marooned in Egypt by Nelson's victory of the Nile. At the same time there was a growth of interest in Britain in establishing quicker communications between the Mediterranean and the Indian Ocean. This interest, however, was chiefly centred on creating speedier overland routes. But the British East India Company, whose gigantic patronage was essential to such schemes, remained doubtful and aloof. There were several reasons for this. To begin with the Company had fallen on hard financial times. Although it ruled British India (in cooperation with the government) it was now more of an administrative organ than a trading company. It seemed unlikely that huge capital investment in the Suez route would pay sufficiently satisfactory rewards. Generally, too, the Company was conservative and distrustful of radical ideas. Nothing was done.

In the early nineteenth century the Age of Steam brought Europe dramatically closer to Asia. It was now possible to reach Alexandria and Suez much more quickly. Interest in the canal was renewed. In 1837, the year of Victoria's accession to the throne, Thomas Waghorn's two-year-old Overland Mail was officially recognised and used by the East India Company. Although this brought Calcutta nearer to London, the cost of a letter between them was exorbitantly high at 5s 5d.

The subsequent decades belonged to the gigantic energies of the Frenchman Ferdinand de Lesseps. This remarkable man, convinced of the necessity for a canal through the Suez Isthmus, campaigned ceaselessly to achieve his object. Although rather naïve in financial matters, de Lesseps was a born publicist, endlessly resourceful, and imaginative. In 1854 he began to form a company to build the canal, and in 1858 saw it formally launched.

But the obstacles in de Lesseps' way were formidable. Not only was there the question of financing the project, but there was also the powerful diplomatic opposition of Great Britain. Official British dislike of the proposed canal was consistent to the point of being

The Khedive Ismail. The building of the Suez Canal bankrupted Ismail and put his dynasty in pawn to European creditors.

fanatical. This was odd, since of all nations Britain, with her vast Asian empire and her widespread commercial activities east of Suez, stood to benefit most from speedier communication between the Mediterranean and the Indian Ocean. British businessmen saw this quite clearly, and a good many of them were enthusiastic supporters of de Lesseps. At the governmental level, however, grave doubts remained.

Led by the forthright and dogmatic Lord Palmerston, British opposition centred on a desire to preserve the status quo in the Middle East. Above all, the French, for so long Britain's main colonial rivals, must be denied a supreme position in the eastern Mediterranean. The Ottoman Empire, ramshackle and inefficient, must be propped up by Britain in order to keep both France and Russia from plundering its choicest parts. To this end, the British ambassador in Istanbul, the leonine Stratford Canning, threw his considerable weight against the Suez Canal Company. The spectre that was haunting the British government was perfectly plain. They feared that, through the Canal Company, France was going to take over the short route to Asia.

Other doubts were of a more mundane nature. It was argued that the cost of building the canal would be prohibitive, and (amazingly) that the different levels between the Mediterranean and Red Seas would lead to disaster. Some insisted that the days of canals were over, and that the railway was the supreme new means of communication. These doubts were partly countered by the impact of the 1857 Indian Mutiny. The British government was acutely embarrassed by the rebellion of a few thousand Indian soldiers of the Bengal army.

The Suez Canal before the water went in.

Strategists were quick to point out that if a Suez Canal had existed in 1857, troops could have been sent more speedily to India and the rising suppressed sooner.

British antagonism, however, continued. Diplomatic intrigue went on unabated. And in 1863, with the canal half built, Britain scored a victory. Armed with evidence that the Canal Company had so far used over 60,000 forced labourers in its work, the British ambassador in Istanbul persuaded the Turkish Sultan to order the Khedive Ismail to halt the digging. Since the Khedive was technically the Sultan's Egyptian Viceroy, this instruction had to be complied with. Morally, of course, there was much to criticise in the recruitment and treatment of Egyptian labour; the European overseers were often heavy-handed, and vehemently regretted that they could not beat their workers at will. Britain's intervention in this matter was, however, less concerned with humanitarianism than with diplomatic advantage.

So powerful was British influence, that work on the canal did not restart properly until 1866, when the Sultan authorised the completion of the project. Ironically, however, British opposition forced the French government to play a more authoritative role in the whole affair. As early as 1860 de Lesseps had appealed to the French Emperor Napoleon III for support. His appeal was perhaps strengthened by the fact that the Empress Eugénie was his cousin. At any rate, French interests dictated a positive intervention. In the wake of the British diplomatic triumph of 1863, the French government in 1864 finally and officially backed the Canal and promised to provide financial support for the Company. Once the Sultan had withdrawn his ban on the digging, de Lesseps could press ahead to his final victory.

This came in December 1869 when the Canal was completed and formally opened. Amid scenes of lavish ceremonial and expensive junketing the representatives of many nations celebrated the opening of a new age of maritime communication. There were some impressive statistics to digest together with the *Poisson à la Réunion des Deux Mers* and the *Crevettes de Suez au Cresson*: the Canal was 100 miles long, 300 feet wide at its surface, and 75,000,000 cubic metres of earth had

The opening of the Suez Canal by the Empress Eugénie in November 1869. The opening was the occasion for spectacular and extravagant ceremonials.

been shifted to build it. But in a tumult of acrobats, fireworks, and belly-dancers some of the harsher realities of the situation were set aside.

These realities, however, soon asserted themselves. The existence of the Canal was bound fundamentally to alter British policy towards the eastern Mediterranean in general and towards Egypt in particular. For how long could Britain refrain from direct intervention? How was France to play her new part in the affairs of the Middle East? Would incipient Egyptian nationalism baulk at the excessive European influence implied by the existence of the powerful Canal Company? Above all how was the Khedive going to steer clear of entanglement in European credit arrangements, and avoid pressure from European nations? All these problems were immediately heightened by the simple fact that the building of the Canal had virtually bankrupted the Khedive. By sanctioning its construction the Egyptian government was soon to find itself in the grip of the most powerful nation of the nineteenth century.

6 Imperial Order and Disorder

Inter-imperial relations; some bonds of Empire; the prospects of dissolution; Chamberlain and the cause of imperial unity; the defence of the Empire; imperial trade, and tariff reform; the Colonial Conference, and the realities of imperial co-operation.

THE LATE-VICTORIAN EMPIRE grew so fast and assumed such complexity that it defied concise definition. In many ways, indeed, it was characterised more by variety than by order. While some imperial theorists could thus draw comforting equations between diversity and strength (even between diversity and democracy), others were appalled, and strove to impose an acceptable pattern on the components of the Empire. The Empire, however, could not be knocked into a uniform shape, though it was possible to smooth out some of the worst irregularities.

The Empire could, of course, be divided into certain groupings. First there were the self-governing colonies, acknowledging the British monarch as their sovereign and still theoretically restricted in a few trivial constitutional fields by the oversight of the Parliament at Westminster. But in practical terms the self-governing colonies really were internally *self-governing*. Their external defence and foreign policy, however, were in Britain's hands, and it was in these areas that the efforts of imperial unionists could be concentrated.

Joseph Chamberlain (1836–1914). Birmingham businessman, Radical, and Imperialist. His tenure of the Colonial Office (1895–1903) was marked by a strenuous attempt to achieve a greater degree of imperial order and cooperation.

Next, the dependency of India (formally created an Empire in 1876) offered at least a geographical and administrative coherence of some sort. There was, to be sure, the dichotomy between British India and the India of the Princes, as well as striking contrasts between different provinces, but overall India could be treated as a unit. The Viceroy, the provincial governors, the Indian Civil Service were all weighty parts of the complicated but functioning machinery of the Raj.

The colonial empire was by 1901 a hotch-potch of possessions. There were Crown Colonies (like Ceylon, Jamaica or Trinidad) ruled by the Colonial Office through a Governor, who was sometimes assisted by Executive and Legislative Councils. Then there were protectorates (such as Uganda, Nyasaland or Aden) mostly ruled by the Foreign Office and often maintaining local institutions. The protected states were one stage removed from protectorates in that indigenous rulers remained in office but were subject to the advice of powerful British Residents. This meant that the protected states (from friendly Tonga to strategically vital Egypt) were also a Foreign Office responsibility. Again, there were the chartered territories (like Rhodesia and North Borneo) which were governed by chartered companies which were allowed virtually a free hand. The Empire also contained two condominiums in the Sudan and the New Hebrides, which were ruled jointly with Egypt and France respectively.

The links of Empire were thus few and far between. At the centre of it all there was, of course, the British crown. The monarch was Queen not only of the United Kingdom, but also of all the self-governing colonies. She

The crown as a bond of Empire. Royal visit of H.R.H. the Duke of Edinburgh (leaning, centre, holding black top hat) to Ceylon. With Victoria a mourning recluse, her sons represented the monarchy on trips to the distant Empire.

Disraeli embarking, with Queen Victoria, on the dangerous waters of imperialism.

Imperial bard.
Rudyard Kipling with
India on the brain.

was Empress of India, and elsewhere a focal point of allegiance and respect, if not always of love. It should not be supposed that a dyak in Borneo, or a Hausa in northern Nigeria, had as clear a picture of the distant monarch as a citizen of Vancouver or Adelaide. Nonetheless, the authority bestowed by the crown was apparent in the deportment of its representatives, from Viceroy to District Officer.

Parliament provided another bond of Empire. But here the link was legalistic and sometimes slipshod. Although a majority at Westminster could overthrow a Governor-General, vote money for a punitive expedition, or even alter the constitution of a self-governing colony, in many ways power continued to be held by the administrators of Empire – the men on the spot. Partly because it was aware of this, partly because imperial issues were generally low on most M.P.'s list of priorities, Parliament held the reins of Empire lightly. So lightly, in fact, that few tended to notice when dextrous executive hands whisked the reins away.

English law also touched the component parts of the Empire. Each one of the Queen's subjects could avail themselves of the apparatus of civil justice. The fact that millions had a very hazy idea of such matters was beside the point. Equality before the law theoretically existed. Although the British might codify and amend,

local laws (unless completely unpalatable) were retained to operate within the mighty framework of English Common Law. At the summit of this legal system was the Judicial Committee of the Privy Council, which acted as a Final Court of Appeal for the whole Empire.

The civil servants of the Empire also lent a degree of uniformity to widely scattered administrations. In the first rank stood the god-like members of the Indian Civil Service, with their high level of academic attainment and their compulsory knowledge of one Indian language, Indian history, and Moslem or Hindu civil law. Recruits to the administrations of the Crown Colonies were perhaps not so high-powered, but they shared similar social backgrounds and had undergone similar educational disciplines. In this respect, the old school tie provided a genuine bond of Empire.

It was of course possible to argue that the only realistic imperial link for the bulk of the Empire was British over-lordship. The dependent territories were thus united in bondage rather than with bonds. The self-governing colonies, however, were free of such subordination. They would cooperate with the mother country when, and how, they saw fit. They could not be ordered into obedience, although they might, on the other hand, be wooed. It was inevitable, therefore, that talk of imperial unity concentrated almost exclusively

An Oriental Ascot. The Happy Valley Racecourse, Hong Kong. If trade did not always follow the flag, British sports certainly did.

Spithead Review, Diamond Jubilee 1897. The British Lion's pride was somewhat misplaced, Canada contributed nothing to the upkeep of the Royal Navy and the Cape had only just begun to do so.

on the relations between Britain and the self-governing
colonies.

Academic and political propagandists reflected this
concern. Seeley's *Expansion of England*, Froude's *Oceana*,
and Dilke's *Greater Britain* were powerful exhortations.
The Imperial Federation League was founded in 1884.
These years also saw the rise of the most dynamic and
persuasive advocate of greater imperial unity – Joseph
Chamberlain (Colonial Secretary 1895–1903). Chamberlain, with his Radical, Nonconformist background,
his political dash and style, had emerged by the end of
Victoria's reign as the imperial knight errant. He
pursued relentlessly the elusive grail of imperial cooperation. In the quest he was prepared to break
political fences, destroy party disciplines, forge new
political alliances. Unfortunately he was also apt, like
Don Quixote, to tilt at windmills.

Chamberlain channelled his efforts for greater unity
into schemes for improving cooperation in the field of
defence and for re-structuring imperial trade. He also
entertained hopes that through the establishment of
bodies such as Imperial Councils, or Parliaments, the

governments of Britain and the self-governing colonies would be able to consult each other regularly and at the highest level. For much of the time it was not quite clear which of these schemes were central to Chamberlain's main purpose, and which were ancillary. Perhaps Chamberlain himself did not know until he had explored fully the various possibilities. The last twenty years of Victoria's reign, however, were to assert the realities of the situation.

Imperial defence seemed to offer a fertile area for experiment. The issues involved were also practical and, to a certain extent, urgent. By the early 1870's local defence was in the hands of the self-governing colonies, although in an emergency British help might be essential. The Second Maori War had demonstrated this, and events in South Africa were to provide even clearer proof. It seemed appropriate, in the circumstances, to organise some degree of inter-imperial defence planning and cooperation as regards the land forces of the Empire.

There were, unfortunately, several colossal drawbacks to these aspirations. First, the British Army and the Royal Navy were by no means willing partners; their senior staff tended to view their opposite numbers with suspicion, even occasionally with hostility. Amazing though it may seem, before the end of the nineteenth century neither service was anxious to let the other know details of its strategic planning. Secondly, the colonies were extremely reluctant to commit themselves to any military arrangement that might prove embarrassing and inappropriate.

The naval defence of the Empire was another matter. The maintenance of squadrons of the Royal Navy in Australasian and South African waters was a costly business. The British government was therefore justified in asking for some contribution to the maintenance of the navy. In 1887, as a result of discussions during the Golden Jubilee celebrations, the Australian colonies and New Zealand agreed to make annual payments for the upkeep of the Royal Navy. In the first year, £850,000 was appropriated.

This innovation, however, owed more to self-interest than to imperial patriotism. The Australasian colonies

J.C.D

Imperial defence. With the self-governing colonies unwilling to commit themselves to elaborate defence schemes, frequent recourse was had to the Indian army. Here, Indian troops are landed at Malta in response to the Russian war scare of 1877.

were isolated settlements on the fringe of the Asian land mass. The surging power of Japan, and the heavy (if demonstrably inefficient) presence of Russia in the East, heightened this isolation. The colonies were buying a measure of security. By 1897 the Cape also contributed to the navy's upkeep. Once more, the gesture was timely in view of the growing crisis in South Africa. By 1902 Natal, too, had joined the subscribers. Canada, however, secure under the mighty wing of the United States, did not pay out one penny, and even spoke of establishing a navy of her own.

One other way of improving defence cooperation lay in establishing appropriate committees. Failing this, the final responsibility for defence planning was borne by the Cabinet, a body frequently ill-equipped to give precise consideration to such matters. A Colonial Defence Committee was created in 1878 in response to the Russian war scare. But it was a feeble body and expired within a year. The Salisbury government of 1885 revived it, however, and it continued to collect and circulate information. In 1890 a Joint Naval and Military Defence Committee was established, but, bedevilled by inter-service disputes, its work lacked clarity or distinction.

The Unionist election victory of 1895 brought a further innovation. This was the establishment of the Cabinet Defence Committee, largely due to a powerful service lobby in the House of Commons, and to the advocacy of Arthur Balfour (Lord Salisbury's nephew and lieutenant). The Defence Committee, however, lacked real authority, and was conspicuous for the absence from its deliberations of the Prime Minister, the Foreign and Colonial Secretaries, and even of the professional heads of the armed services. No minutes were kept, and the Committee's work remained generally ill-defined and ineffective.

The military fiascos of the Boer War of 1899–1902 did a great deal to destroy this erratic approach towards imperial defence. The end of the war coincided with the accession of Balfour to the Premiership. Impelled by his own conviction, and prodded by his service ministers, Balfour duly reconstituted the Cabinet Defence Committee. The new body was chaired by the Prime Minister himself and included the Secretary for War, and the First Lord of the Admiralty, as well as the First Sea Lord, the Commander-in-Chief, and the heads of Naval and Military Intelligence.

By 1904 the committee had been transformed into the Committee of Imperial Defence. It had a permanent secretariat (a revolutionary step) and was able to invite any minister, service expert or colonial statesman to its meetings. It was essentially an advisory body, but a powerful one because of its membership. Balfour was optimistic over its potential, and particularly cherished the hope that it would speedily become a really effective vehicle for cooperation between Britain and the self-governing colonies. Although these aspirations were not totally fulfilled, the precedent that had been established was a healthy one.

Imperial trade seemed to be another promising basis

for improved cooperation. By the end of the century a little less than a third of Britain's trade was with the Empire. The principles of free trade dominated British economic theory. This meant, among other things, that if Britain had already signed a commercial treaty with Germany and subsequently concluded a further agreement with (say) Canada, then Germany too could expect similar preferential terms with Canada. In these circumstances, imperial loyalties were less significant than fiscal realities. In general terms, Britain made plain her wish to buy in the cheapest market and to sell in the dearest.

With the whole world as her oyster it seemed at first sight unlikely that Britain would lightly abandon the advantage of free trade. But from 1870 onwards the mid-Victorian boom began to fade. British exports suffered alarming fluctuations, and there were severe bouts of commercial depression and unemployment. Other nations, notably Germany and the United States, were expanding their industries on a scale which threatened eventually to overtake Britain's early lead. By the 1890's most of the major manufacturing countries had adopted some measure of protection. Britain alone clung to free trade.

Faced with these facts, there were some who began to press for the adoption of tariff reform. By 1902 Joseph Chamberlain had become convinced that through tariff reform Britain would not only be assured of her place in the sun of economic growth, but could also hope to bring the self-governing colonies and herself into more intimate cooperation. Frustrated in his plans for im-

Chamberlain's difficulty in selling Tariff Reform. Joe: 'Now then, gents, you may think this loaf is a little 'un, but you just look at it through these patent Imperial Protection double magnifying spectacles!'
The Working Man: 'That's all very well, mister, but we want to *eat* the loaf, not look at it'.

perial councils and for precise schemes of imperial defence, Chamberlain sought to combine economic self-interest with calls for imperial unity.

An imperial common market, however, was beyond reach. The self-governing colonies still wanted to protect their infant industries; British politicians feared the electoral consequences of taking in dearer colonial food. Colonial markets were in any case too small for British manufactures. The best that could reasonably be achieved was a lowering of tariff barriers against imperial goods, although in practice preference might also be given by raising tariffs against the foreigner. This was the underlying principle of tariff reform.

One promising development had been the $33\frac{1}{3}\%$ preference given by Canada to British manufactures between 1897 and 1900. The British government, however, was unable to make any effective response. There had apparently been a momentary triumph for Chamberlain when the Cabinet agreed in 1902 to impose a duty on imported corn, meal and flour. It was now possible to exempt the self-governing colonies from this Corn Tax. Canada in particular would then receive reciprocal preferential treatment. Unfortunately for Chamberlain, free trade orthodoxy at the Treasury, embodied in the resolute Chancellor of the Exchequer, C. T. Ritchie, swept away the Corn Tax and with it all immediate hopes for tariff reform.

Chamberlain responded to this setback by throwing

the tariff reform issue before the public for debate. Controversy divided the Cabinet, and in September 1903 not only Chamberlain but also four free trade ministers resigned. With Balfour's tacit blessing, Chamberlain now launched his ambitious, well-heeled, but divisive Tariff Reform Campaign. Between 1903 and the General Election of 1906, the Campaign ground on. It shattered the unity of the Unionist party, and, although effective in a few areas, offered a glorious target for the staunchly free trade Liberals. The election of 1906 decimated the Unionists and returned a Liberal government with a huge majority.

The Liberals would not countenance tariff reform and Chamberlain's plans had suffered a prodigious blow. In the wilderness, however, the Unionists became increasingly committed to tariff reform. But although colonial governments showed fairly steady interest in imperial preference, British statesmen were wary of the 'dear bread' cry, and reluctant to offend the electorate. When eventually imperial preference was introduced in 1932, it was in response to the faltering of world trade during the Great Slump. Imperial patriotism, as perhaps Chamberlain had always suspected, flourished best on a diet of economic self-interest.

Plans for imperial federation also remained unfulfilled. Although there were enthusiastic exponents of federation in Britain and the self-governing colonies, the practical difficulties were enormous. What subjects were to be reserved for the proposed Imperial Assembly? How was it possible to avoid clashes over sovereignty between the central legislature and local parliaments? Above all, how was the Federal Parliament to be composed? If delegates were elected on the basis of proportional representation, then the British members would swamp those from the self-governing colonies. Having recently attained the substance of domestic autonomy, the self-governing colonies were unlikely to throw away their independence in this fashion.

Faced with these problems, Britain and her self-governing colonies reached a typically pragmatic compromise. Like the majority of such agreements, the result was uncontroversial, reasonable, economical, and not particularly efficient. Instead of creating an Im-

Diamond Jubilee in Penang. Ceremonial arch in Beach Street.

perial Federal Parliament, the Empire made use of the
Colonial Conference. The first of these had met at the
time of Queen Victoria's Golden Jubilee celebrations
in 1887. It had seemed convenient for the assembled
colonial Prime Ministers to consult with the British
government. The precedent was repeated at the Queen's
Diamond Jubilee in 1897. In this way, Her Majesty, by
attaining a ripe old age, contributed much practical
assistance to the better organisation of her Empire.

After 1897 it was agreed to hold Colonial Conferences
at five-yearly intervals. The Conferences were never the
occasions for dynamic decision-making. Although hefty
agendas were discussed, and the delegates ranged freely
over the many topics of common interest, any policy
agreed on by the Conference had then to be vetted by
the local colonial legislatures. Colonial autonomy thus
remained intact. In other words, the Colonial Conferences could only be as useful as the delegates wanted
them to be. They were, however, of some symbolic
significance, and the free exchange of opinions doubtless
cleared the diplomatic air a little.

It was also possible to be cynical about the Conferences. John Morley even thought they were in danger
of 'becoming the greatest bore that was ever known'.
Certainly there was something faintly ludicrous about
heads of state attending a conference which had
absolutely no power; just as, despite all the talk about
joint defence and foreign policies, when it came to crisis
point Britain acted solely in her own interests. Persistent
British promises to consult the governments of the self-
governing colonies were equally persistently broken.

But at least the Conferences existed. If nothing else
they demonstrated the clear differences between British
and colonial statesmen. The British Prime Minister
tended (until 1911) to open the proceedings with a lofty
and fairly ritualistic speech and then depart to the care
of more weighty matters. To fill the void, the Colonial
Secretary then chaired the Conference. Between the
British and colonial sides there frequently yawned a
vast gap in social origin, educational opportunity and
cultural attainment. Lord Salisbury, the Earl of Derby,
and Sir Henry Holland (for example) had little in
common with Australian premiers like Henry Parkes or
Alfred Deakin. Joseph Chamberlain, with his business-

Colonial Conference,
1902. Despite Chamber-
lain's efforts, the Con-
ferences of 1897 and 1902
produced no blue-print
for cooperation. *Front row:*
second from left, Seddon
(New Zealand), Laurier
(Canada), Chamberlain,
Barton (Australia).

man's sensibilities, perhaps approached the middle ground, as did the well-groomed Wilfrid Laurier of Canada. Otherwise it is tempting to see a confrontation between sophisticated English statesmen and be-whiskered, thick-booted, colonials. The accents of Eton and Oxford must have jarred against the plainer and more democratic tones of Ontario and Queensland.

But the most fundamental problem dogging the cause of imperial unity was the irreversible growth of colonial nationalism. When British interests coincided with those of the self-governing colonies, then cooperation was possible against a background of flag-wagging and hearty renderings of *Rule Britannia*! When, however, these interests were at odds, a rather dogged dialogue ensued. It was to the credit of more detached statesmen, such as Salisbury and Balfour, that these facts were appreciated.

Given this perception, the more realistic course was to fasten on to those links that already existed rather than to forge new ones. The existing bonds of Empire, though unrestrictive, were not without strength. A common monarch, a shared history, a common law, similar institutions, and a sense of cultural identity were the bones of the body imperial. Imperfect though these links were, they were at least organic growths rather than the result of hasty grafting. Loyalty was better than an alliance, a set of common interests more reliable than a tripartite treaty. Thus constructed, the relationship between Britain and her self-governing colonies was to prove capable of the most remarkable endurance.

7 The Emergence of the Dominions

Britain and the self-governing colonies.

CANADA: *problems of central and provincial government; the Canadian Pacific railway, and expansion; new immigrants; the twin pulls of Britain and the United States; Laurier and Canada's identity.*

AUSTRALIA: *boom in the 1880's; developing nationalism; 'the white Australia' policy; the quest for federation; the 1890's slump; the establishment of the Commonwealth of Australia, 1901.*

NEW ZEALAND: *a distinct identity; opts out of Australian federation; the lack of an independent foreign policy; establishment of a welfare state; some local leaders: Vogel, Reeves and Seddon.*

THE YEARS 1870 to 1901 saw the self-governing colonies grow in population, prosperity and confidence. By the end of Victoria's reign they had attained, in all but name, the status of independent nations: perhaps only third-class nations, but recognisable all the same. They thus occupied a somewhat ambiguous place within the legalistic unity of the British Empire. The British government, by a declaration of war, could theoretically commit the whole Empire to hostilities; yet the degree of participation in any such war was at the discretion of the self-governing colonies. Britain could sign treaties and conclude alliances on behalf of the Empire; but she could not compel the self-governing colonies to honour these agreements.

Put in the plainest terms, there were a considerable number of instances when British and colonial interests were at odds. Some formula was therefore needed which would maintain the constitutional harmony of the Empire while acknowledging local differences. Although no official recipe for this problem had emerged by 1901, in practice the British government dealt tactfully with the susceptibilities of the self-governing

Symbol and means of growth. The last spike driven into the Canadian Pacific Railway on 7 November 1885. Montreal was now linked to Vancouver.

colonies. Those statesmen, like Joseph Chamberlain, who tried to blast the colonies into closer cooperation with the mother country were untypical. Despite their common allegiance to the crown, despite their acceptance that foreign policy would be made in Westminster, the self-governing colonies between 1870 and 1901 were indeed nations in the making.

The Canadian federation survived the early trials of provincial antipathies and the problems inherent in a newly-established central government. The only alternative, indeed, to cooperation was sterile particularism leading very probably to undue interference from the United States. Faced with this prospect, and sustained by the flexible principles of British parliamentary practice, the Canadian people sought unity as the corollary to provincial well-being. The foundations of unity were to include the binding together of the scattered geographical units of the nation, and the direction of economic expansion by the federal government.

In the 1870's three new provinces entered the Confederation. These were Manitoba (1870), British Columbia (1871) and Prince Edward Island (1873). By 1905 the prairie provinces of Saskatchewan and Alberta had joined. As early as 1880 the Canadian government had taken over all British possessions in North America, with the exception of Newfoundland. The government at Ottawa was now master of a united Canada stretching from the Atlantic to the Pacific.

But although united by one constitution, Canada was still a skeleton of a nation geographically. There were substantial numbers of citizens in Quebec, Ontario and the Maritimes, and a healthy clump in British Columbia. But elsewhere the population belt, sticking close to the United States border, was perilously thin. The Canadian wasteland dominated the settlements. Any distance north of the border, the winter dominated the wasteland.

The railways, however, offered hope for the future. The great Canadian Pacific line was opened in 1885. Financed in the main from London, but also aided by

Dominion government grants of money and land, the Canadian Pacific became virtually an estate of the realm. It alone carried essential freight across an almost empty continent; it alone was capable of ferrying members to the Parliament at Ottawa; it alone, for immense distances of prairie and forest, stood for civilisation and progress, a symbol of man's determination to get the better of his environment.

Other railways, branching off from the great trunk of the Canadian Pacific, helped to close the gaps between settlements, and provided the vehicles of economic growth. Homesteaders and lumbermen pushed north and west. District after district fell to the plough. New strains of wheat were bred to ripen quickly and withstand the harsh climate. The 1880's and 90's were years of growing prosperity, even of a mild boom. Towns flourished in this optimistic atmosphere. Between 1871 and 1891 the population of Toronto leapt from 56,000 to some 180,000; land prices rocketed accordingly. Montreal, the chief import-export city of British North America, had about 200,000 inhabitants at the 1891 census. This widespread urban growth, however, was often at the expense of the rural districts. It did not mean that the Canadian population was overall increasing at such a dramatic rate.

The influx of immigrants in the last quarter of the nineteenth century was nonetheless encouraging. British emigration societies (of which there were 28 in 1901) were generally careful and responsible in their activities. They vetted prospective migrants, tried to ensure that jobs were waiting for them in Canada, and sometimes

kept an eye on them afterwards. Large sections of the Canadian public, however, were appalled at the prospect of continuing massive immigration from Ireland. This attitude was founded not only on trade union fears of a glut on certain labour markets, but also on simple prejudice. The Irish poor, who in fact deserved the most sympathetic consideration, were stereotyped as ignorant drunkards, diseased and pauperised, a threat to the morals of Canadian society.

Predictably, immigrants were accused of causing epidemics, and filling gaols and asylums. It was certainly true that fairly large numbers of recent immigrants could be found in such institutions, but in many cases this was no more than an illustration that they had fled from gross hardship and chronic underprivilege in their countries of origin. In many ways Canada could not afford to be so choosy over her future citizens. By the 1890's she was not drawing enough immigrants from the preferred countries of Britain and northern Europe. Accompanied by yet another chorus of criticism, the Canadian government decided to turn to southern and eastern Europe. In 1901 roughly seventy per cent of new immigrants came from the Austrian empire,

Italy, Russia and Poland.

This was to have a significant, though at first small-scale, effect on the character of the Canadian population. In 1871, ninety-two per cent of Canada's citizens were of British and French origin. Within this context the British outnumbered the French by 2 to 1. But between 1871 and 1911 the Anglo-French proportion of the population dropped by nine per cent. It seemed therefore that Canada, like the United States, was destined to become racially diverse while retaining the fabric of Anglo-Saxon institutions and culture. Some of the new immigrant groups, however, stood like granite outcrops in the sea of English-speaking Canada. The Mennonite settlements in Manitoba were puritanically sincere, theocratic societies. The Doukhobors of Saskatchewan were persecuted peasant refugees from Tsarist Russia; pacifist and communistic, such groups were oddities in a country that was happily large enough and empty enough to contain them.

In other respects, Canadian society in the last decades of the nineteenth century balanced (not always elegantly) between the twin pulls of Britain and the United States. The growth of great cities could have brought the American diseases of civic corruption and organised crime to Canada. Although by no means entirely free from these abuses, the Canadian cities were able to keep a staunch check on them. Toronto, Montreal and Vancouver thus had more in common with Manchester than with Chicago. If the towns were relatively clear of hoodlum gangs, the prairies also seem to have had fewer sharp-shooting criminals than the American West.

On the other hand, Canada was plainly North American. Public libraries sprang up in the towns, and an eager interest was expressed in scientific and technical education. The civic authorities were perhaps excessively severe on personal vices. Prostitution was harried by a vigilant police force. The taking of tobacco and alcohol was actively discouraged. Although Canada could claim (with others) to be the land of the free, there were in practice fairly strict limitations on the smaller freedoms.

Politically, too, Canada had an ambiguous position. Unsure of her identity, she was only sure of what she

New Canadians.
A Mennonite settlement in Manitoba in the 1880's.

did not want. High on this list of negatives was her determination to avoid subordination to either Great Britain or the United States. Although Americans were suspicious that Canada was merely a British colony, Canadian statesmen were adamant that this was not the case. Even the traditionally loyalist, Anglo-Saxon, anti-Catholic, Conservative party was clear on this point. Its leader, the rip-roaring Sir John Macdonald, though proud of the imperial connection, was a passionate nationalist, little inclined to involve Canada in Britain's far-flung colonial problems. After 1896 the Liberals were in power and led by the urbane, fastidious, and subtle Wilfrid Laurier. As a French-Canadian, and equally as leader of the anti-imperialist Liberal party, Laurier was in no position slavishly to follow the Union Jack.

Ironically, however, Laurier's premiership gave heart to British Imperial Federalists. Although extremely difficult to pin down to any firm commitment, Laurier took certain steps towards the flamboyant positions held by Joseph Chamberlain. The preferential treatment offered to British exporters between 1897 and 1900 was one such step. So was the favourable Canadian response to Chamberlain's tariff reform aspirations at the Colonial Conference of 1902. It could, of course, be argued that economic self-interest was the dominant factor in these moves. But during the Boer War, Laurier let Canadian volunteers serve in South Africa, even if he was loath to dispatch regular troops.

Under Laurier, Canada achieved something of that internal harmony which had for so long eluded her. Laurier's career, indeed, was symbolic of the need to reconcile French particularism with the wider prospect of a Canadian nation. Thus Laurier, the Anglicised French-Canadian, took a knighthood from the hands of the Queen-Empress at the Diamond Jubilee of 1897. His lack of separatist fanaticism reassured English-speaking Canadians; the fact that he was French comforted the citizens of Quebec.

It was true that self-governing Newfoundland found little incentive to join the Canadian federation, and sometimes expressed fears of Canadian intentions towards her. To other eyes Canada looked less fearsome. Not a colony, not yet a nation; not completely

Sir John A. MacDonald,
Tory Prime Minister of
Canada.

Sir Wilfrid Laurier,
Liberal Prime Minister
(1896–1911). As a French-
Canadian Prime
Minister, Laurier was
uniquely placed to
encourage national unity.

British, not yet Americanised. The land was beset with contradictions. Laurier made bold enough to claim that the twentieth century would belong to Canada. If events have proved him wrong, it was nevertheless essential to have invested such confidence in the Canadian future.

Bales of wool, one of the Australian colonies' major exports, on the road to the docks.

AUSTRALIA

Between 1870 and 1901 the Australian colonies enjoyed a runaway boom, saw it broken, and entered the new century as a single constitutional unit – the Commonwealth of Australia. Until about 1890, Australia's development was at break-neck speed. Immigrants were plentiful, the seasons benevolent, the land profitable enough to encourage heavy overseas investment. For a time there seemed no limit to Australian expansion.

To a certain extent the boom was engineered by political strategists. After the stagnation of the 1870's

Weight : 630 lbs
Height : 4 ft. 9 in.
Width : 2 ft. 2 in.
average thickness 4 inches
Value £12000..

Bernard Holtermann, co-discoverer of the largest nugget of reef gold to be taken from the earth. The discovery was made at Hill End, New South Wales.

political platforms began to ring with cries for massive local spending on railways, public works and social services. In New South Wales the Governor, Sir Hercules Robinson, argued that the government should build fifty miles of railway every year. Politicians and electorate agreed. Between 1871 and 1891 nearly 10,000 miles of railway were added to the meagre 1,000 that had previously served all the Australian colonies. Telegraph lines multiplied prodigously, and tens of thousands of pounds were spent on local irrigation schemes.

In the 1880's important mineral discoveries also boosted investment in Australia. Gold, copper, lead, silver and zinc deposits were unearthed in New South Wales, Queensland and Tasmania. The coal industry was greatly stimulated. Money poured into Australian land and wool. After 1880 the use of refrigerated ships led to a healthy export trade in frozen meat. The Queensland sugar plantations prospered, though at the

137

expense of the thousands of Kanakas, imported coloured labour from the South Seas; 'black-birding' continued, despite local and Imperial insistence that it was covert slavery, until the end of the century.

The boom was attended by the strong growth of Australian nationalism. The relatively high standard of living enjoyed by most citizens went hand in hand with an egalitarian, even radical, approach to social development. The hard line adopted by a good many in the trade union movement not only gave Australian labour a reputation for stubbornness and bite, but also guaranteed a fairer share of profits. Notions of class superiority and snobbery generally found short shrift. Despite its division into separate colonies Australia, by the 1890's, was capable of exhibiting strong nationalist traits. Rather like American patriotism, Australian nationalism was based on the firm conviction that here was a country to be proud of; a land of the free, a land of prosperity.

There were, however, some ugly overtones to all this.

Australian prejudice against cheap Chinese labour. Part of a cartoon sequence showing a Chinaman manufacturing dingo tails in order to claim a six-fold reward!

Most striking was the intolerance shown towards non-Europeans. By 1871 there were about 25,000 Chinese in Australia, brought over to work on the goldfields. Occasional riots and persistent agitation against them led to all the colonies passing discriminatory legislation by the end of the century. The heavy fees thus imposed on prospective non-European immigrants in general reflected the fears and prejudices of working-class Australia. The growth of Labour owed little to Marxist principles of international socialism, much more to trade union solidarity embellished by the ideals of John Stuart Mill. It was thus possible to support both discrimination on the grounds of race, and schemes of social welfare.

This defensive attitude towards Australia's identity was frequently extended to external affairs. Even royalists were sometimes exasperated by disinterested behaviour on the part of Britain. The vetoing of Queensland's annexation of New Guinea, the refusal to take seriously Australian fears of German expansion in the Pacific, were causes of sharp resentment. More radical observers of British imperial policy were incensed by examples of aggression in the Sudan or South Africa. One remedy, it was argued, lay in the closer consultation which imperial federation would bring. A more realistic remedy was for Australia to federate herself, and thus assume the appearance of a united nation entitled to international respect.

Australian federation, however, was not so easily achieved. At first sight, it seemed a logical enough step. The colonies enjoyed a homogenous racial character, and practised similar constitutional methods. The emergence of Germany as a power in the Pacific encouraged Australians to consider the strength that federation would bring. Henry Parkes of New South Wales and Alfred Deakin of Victoria were persuasive and persistent advocates.

Despite these factors, the federation movement dragged on for thirty years. Inter-colonial rivalries died hard. Local politicians cherished their authority, and were jealous of the assumptions of federal government. The economic interests of the colonies were by no means compatible, and a fairly rigorous tariff system separated them. Western Australia (which did not obtain responsible government until 1893) and Queensland were of separatist convictions. In addition, the increasingly powerful colonial Labour parties were more concerned with reforms at home than with an ambitious Australian intervention in the South Seas.

The disastrous slump of the early 1890's, however, reinforced the federalist case. In a little over a decade, less than 3,000,000 Australians had borrowed nearly £200,000,000. Credit now collapsed. The almost insane land boom was broken. Confidence in expensive public works was shattered. The economic crisis curbed the more extravagant claims for Australia's future. It helped to transform polite lip-service to federal ideals into a programme with a real chance of success. Strength might indeed come from unity.

Inter-colonial conferences, and even the formation of a Federal Council in 1885, produced no concrete step until 1897. In that year representatives of five Australian colonies began to draft a federal constitution. Queensland and New Zealand took no part in this process. By early 1900, however, the proposed constitution had been accepted in referenda in all the mainland colonies save Western Australia. Within a few months Western Australia, wooed by the Colonial Secretary Joseph Chamberlain, and with its voting tilted towards federation by the miners of the new goldfields, had dropped its separatist attitude. New Zealand decided to remain independent of the whole business.

The twentieth century thus opened neatly with the passing of the Australian Commonwealth Act in the British Parliament. In significant details the Australian federation was unlike the Canadian, more like the constitution of the United States, although the powers of the federal and state governments were the subject of clear demarcation. The Lower Chamber (in which seats were to be automatically redistributed) was called the House of Representatives; the elected Senate, which represented the states, was given considerable authority.

In some ways the new constitution was strikingly radical. Differences between the two federal chambers, and proposed amendments to the constitution, were to be resolved by the will of the majority in Parliament and submission to the people in a referendum. The use of the referendum had been basic to the construction of the

Alfred Deakin (1856–1919). Statesman from Victoria; supporter both of Chamberlain's plans for imperial unity, and of Australian federation.

federation and was to remain an essentially democratic feature of the new Commonwealth. Even the term 'Commonwealth' was in tune with the egalitarian qualities of Australian society. The constitution-makers were also determined that the Governor-General should play no more than a modest discretionary role.

The Commonwealth of Australia came formally into being on 1 January 1901. A compromise capital had to be built at Canberra in federal territory in order to offend neither New South Wales nor Victoria. This decision owed something to the example of Washington, D.C., balancing between the American North and South. The new country, although occasionally subject to bouts of rabid nationalism, was in effect dependent on Britain for her external defence. This meant that

Australia was generally a loyal supporter of British foreign policy. Thus while Australian politics saw the early emergence of Labour governments, the country's response to the outside world tended to be rather conservative. Complete independence was evidently many years away.

Although New Zealand was a geographical partner of Australia in her isolation in the South Seas, the two countries were not necessarily on close terms. The advent of a common foe would naturally have spurred them to joint action. Failing this, however, New Zealand tended to regard the Australian colonies with indifference, if not with hostility. By the end of the century New Zealand statesmen firmly declined to have any part in Australian federation. Paradoxically, far greater enthusiasm was shown for imperial federation.

There were several reasons for this state of affairs. First, New Zealanders by no means saw themselves as part of an Australasian whole. They argued, not without justice, that their island environment, and their different history, gave them a separate identity. Secondly, in any federation worthy of the name there would be crucial issues reserved for the Federal Parliament. The New Zealand representatives would be hopelessly outnumbered in such a Parliament. How could this sort of arrangement best serve New Zealand's interests? Close observers of antipodean politics were thus not particularly surprised when New Zealand opted out of the Australian federation. Anything more than the most superficial survey of the Australasian colonies would have revealed that there was little love lost between Wellington and Sydney.

Indeed, in the last three decades of the Victorian age, New Zealand statesmen argued enthusiastically that their country had a special mission in the South Pacific. It was claimed that New Zealand had a part to play in extending Anglo-Saxon rule and influence in Polynesia. More optimistic was the insistence that a rapidly increasing population would soon turn New Zealand into an antipodean Britain, with a strong navy, and a vigorous imperialism of its own.

In practice these ambitions remained substantially unfulfilled. New Zealand governments had to be content with nagging Britain to take action in the South Seas. The spectre of German and French expansion tended to leave the British government unmoved. Subsequently both Germany and France acquired firm footholds in the Pacific. When, however, war came in 1914 the German colonies were rapidly devoured by New Zealand, Australian and British forces. Thus after half a century of clamouring, New Zealand, largely through the mandate system, received the Polynesian empire she had always considered that she deserved.

Domestic developments were more satisfying. In social reform, late-Victorian New Zealand could claim to lead the whole Empire. Her achievements in this sphere sprang mainly from the equitable and egalitarian nature of her society. To a compact and fairly secure community, the intervention of the state in social and economic matters seemed logical and unobjectionable.

Opening of the First Parliament of the Commonwealth of Australia, 1901, by the Duke of York (later King George v).

There was little high-flown socialist theorising; the bloody banners of insurrection were not raised; the prevailing attitude was practical and just. Although many problems remained unanswered, those that were tackled received humane and progressive treatment.

By 1901 New Zealand had a good deal of pioneering social legislation to her credit. Manhood suffrage had been introduced in 1889. Votes for women (including Maori women) followed in 1893; this was a quarter of a century before British women, aged thirty or more, were given the vote. A free, secular, and compulsory primary school system was set up. Laws were introduced to speed up the settlement of industrial disputes by arbitration, although this by no means ended strike action. A comprehensive set of regulations for industry protected the workers. A non-contributory pensions scheme was introduced. All this meant that by the end of the nineteenth century, New Zealand had established the foundations of a welfare state. Although many scoffed, it was an achievement of which most New Zealanders were deservedly proud.

In some measure, social reform had sprung from the economic depression of the 1880's. Following the collapse of the boom inspired by Julius Vogel's policy of heavy borrowing to finance public works, various New Zealand governments had allayed hardship with welfare measures. This was especially true of the Liberal administration of the 1890's. But this decade also saw the successful launching of the frozen meat industry and the parallel stimulus to dairy farming in the greater export possibilities for butter. Moreover, after the Vogel spree, New Zealand had learnt to live within its means by 1901, and this was a lesson worth the learning.

Despite its mere three quarters of a million citizens by the end of the century, and despite its excessive reliance upon agriculture, New Zealand merited serious treatment as a nation. That narrow-mindedness and provincial attitudes should have existed was inevitable; that forward-looking domestic legislation should have been enacted was not. Formidable leaders had emerged: Vogel with his imagination, dash, and sometimes misplaced optimism; Harry Atkinson with his financial prudence allied to a generous concept of welfare; William Pember Reeves, cultured, eloquent, a thoughtful socialist, who provided the theory behind the welfare measures, and became eventually Director of the London School of Economics.

Finally there was the massive figure of Richard Seddon, Prime Minister from 1893 to 1906. Seddon was homely, direct, and strong. His use of English had more in common with the language of a pioneer community than with the subtleties of diplomatic exchange. He had little use for book learning, and his enemies indeed doubted whether he had ever read a single book. But Seddon represented much that was valuable in New Zealand society. He was unpretentious, canny, and reliable, an appropriate leader for a developing nation.

New Zealand electioneering. Prime Minister Richard Seddon delivering a direct, hard-hitting speech.

8 Southern Africa 1870-1907

Diamonds at Kimberley; the Zulu menace; Disraeli's annexation of the Transvaal; Gladstone and the independence of the Transvaal; Battle of Majuba Hill, 1881; the Rand goldstrike of 1886; the Uitlander problem; Cecil Rhodes and the quest for British supremacy; the Jameson Raid; Chamberlain, Milner and the drive towards war; the Boer War, 1899–1902; disasters, farm-burning, and concentration camps; post-war reconstruction and reform; Botha, Smuts and self-government.

THE DISCOVERY of diamonds at Kimberley in 1869 injected a further element of conflict into southern Africa. Kimberley was in Griqualand West, which was disputed territory between Britain and the Orange Free State. In 1876 the British government eventually bought out the Free State's claims for a mere £90,000. The diamond fields boomed, and a few individuals made their fortunes, among them a sickly youth called Cecil Rhodes. The controversy showed how peaceful pasture land could overnight be transformed into an arena for the conflicting interests of big business and sovereign governments. Kimberley was not the last site in South Africa to receive such treatment.

British policy towards southern Africa in the mid-1870's became generally more active. Although the chief requirement cherished by the British government was that the Cape route should be secure and the Cape hinterland peaceful, this tranquility now seemed threatened. The growing menace of the efficient Zulu *impis* of Chief Cetewayo faced the Transvaal with a massive assault and possibly with annihilation. The return of Lord Carnarvon to the Colonial Office in 1874 meant that colonial policy was now directed by a firm believer in British supremacy throughout southern Africa. Perhaps this could best be achieved through federation between the British colonies and the Afrikaner republics.

In 1876 it looked as if the Transvaal and the Orange

Above Facing the Zulus. British troops at the disastrous battle of Isandhlwana, 1880, where the Zulu *impis* broke the redcoat lines.

The Big Hole at Kimberley. The diamond discoveries at Kimberley made Cecil Rhodes' fortune and pointed to the unearthing of future mineral deposits in southern Africa. At Kimberley the individual diggings were connected to the rim of the Big Hole by thousands of ropes and pulleys.

Free State could be wheedled, or pushed, into federation. Carnarvon put pressure on a reluctant Disraeli to support such a policy. The Colonial Secretary subsequently sent his agent Theophilus Shepstone to the Transvaal in 1877. In Pretoria, Shepstone found the government of President Burgers in desperate financial difficulties; it was almost impossible to wring taxes from the Transvaalers and the Treasury contained 12s 6d. In April 1877, and with Burgers more than half willing, Shepstone proclaimed the annexation of the Transvaal. It seemed that a prodigious step had been taken by Britain.

The long-awaited Zulu War broke out in 1879, prompted by a pugnacious ultimatum from the new Governor of the Cape, Sir Bartle Frere. The war provided the Afrikaners with the spectacle of the early and catastrophic defeat of British arms at the Battle of Isandhlwana. Although the subsequent triumph at Ulundi broke Zulu power for ever, it also removed the most cogent justification for Britain's annexation of the Transvaal – the protection of its citizens. Failure to implement promises of local autonomy further provoked Afrikaner resentments, although hopes for a speedy restoration of their independence were raised by the election victory of Gladstone and the Liberals in 1880.

Once in office, however, Gladstone's policies were rather more ambiguous than his utterances while in opposition. Basically Gladstone rejected South African

148

federation. He sacked Bartle Frere, and stealthily entered into negotiations with the Transvaalers. But no immediate grant of freedom, or of local self-government, came. Taking events in their own hands, the Transvaalers rose in revolt and inflicted a sharp defeat on a small British force at Majuba Hill in 1881. Although possessing the means to reverse this humiliation, Gladstone sensibly decided upon a settlement.

The Pretoria Convention of 1881, which was revised at the Convention of London in 1884, gave the Transvaal its independence. A degree of confusion, however, remained as regards British suzerainty. A clear reference to 'the suzerainty of Her Majesty' in the Convention of 1881 was deleted in the agreement of 1884. Although it was accepted that Britain should have oversight of future treaties between the Transvaal and any other nation (except the Orange Free State), and with African tribes to the east and west, the wider concept of suzerainty remained obscure. Fundamentally, the Transvaal (led after 1883 by the resolute Paul Kruger) denied that suzerainty existed, while the British government would not admit to this. The issue was later to to be revived in dramatic circumstances.

Rout of British arms at Majuba Hill in 1881. This remarkable victory by Boer commandos not only spurred the British government into restoring independence to the Transvaal, but was prophetic of early engagements in the South African War of 1899–1902.

Within two years of the Convention of London, the discovery of gold on the Witwatersrand reef developed into another threat to the recently restored independence of the Transvaal. The problem centred on the influx of thousands of fortune-hunting foreigners, most of whom claimed British citizenship. Within ten years these Uitlanders built up the gold industry, and turned Johannesburg from a sleepy dorp into a thriving city of over 50,000 Europeans. It was soon reckoned that the Uitlanders outnumbered the Transvaalers. Although this was perhaps an exaggeration, Kruger's government had to face certain unpleasant facts.

Chief among these was the possibility that the Uitlanders would turn the Transvaal into a community dominated by its English-speaking citizens. British policy would thus have gained a bloodless victory. Kruger was determined to have none of this. While levying substantial taxes upon the Uitlanders, he refused to admit them to full citizenship. It is not difficult to appreciate Kruger's disquiet at the Uitlander problem. As a small boy he had taken part in the Great Trek; as a rising politician he had seen Disraeli's annexation of the Transvaal. Appreciating the depth of Afrikaner nationalism, Kruger could not countenance a surrender to the larger forces of British imperialism and international finance.

But the Rand goldstrike forced a change in British policy that was every bit as positive as Kruger's dogged insistence on independence. As the Transvaal was transformed from an agricultural backwater into a prosperous state relying upon an expanding industry, a new spectre haunted British policymakers. This was the very real possibility that South African federation would be achieved eventually under the leadership of the Transvaal rather than under the Cape.

British supremacy, however, might prove difficult to assert except through force. Throughout the 1890's, both in Britain and South Africa, more men were obliged to come to this conclusion. By the end of the decade Kruger's government had judiciously purchased a considerable amount of modern weaponry. For its part, the British government, and its supporters in South Africa, extracted the maximum amount of sympathy from the alleged plight of the Uitlander. As long

After Majuba Hill, Transvaal leaders and British officers talk terms at a nearby farm-house. Paul Kruger (left of centre) is doffing his hat. Sir Evelyn Wood (centre) is holding a swagger stick and pith helmet.

Cecil John Rhodes (1853–1902). Self-made millionaire, imperial expansionist, dreamer of dreams, and woman-hater, Rhodes exerted enormous influence over southern Africa in the period 1880 to 1902.

as the Uitlanders were denied civil rights, the British government could claim an interest in the affairs of the Transvaal which exceeded the hazy limits of suzerainty. If this diplomatic offensive failed, there were those who advocated direct intervention.

By 1895 Cecil Rhodes had come to believe in the use of force to bring the Transvaal into a South African federation. Rhodes' influence throughout southern Africa was enormous; his nickname 'the Colossus' had some point to it. He seemed at the height of his political powers. He was backed by the enormous wealth of his great diamond and gold companies. De Beers and Consolidated Goldfields Limited gave him the means to change history. He had already redrawn the map of Africa. It had been Rhodes who had agitated for the annexation of Bechuanaland in 1884 in order to provide the means of by-passing the Transvaal. It had been the troops of Rhodes' British South Africa Company who in 1889, armed with rifles and a Royal Charter, had crossed the Limpopo river and opened up Rhodesia – the counterpoise to the north.

More orthodox had been Rhodes' political man-oeuvres in the Cape. By 1890 he had allied the English-speaking Progressive party with the Afrikaner moderates led by Jan Hofmeyer. This feat brought him the premiership of the self-governing Cape Colony, and was consistent with his desire to woo the Afrikaners into

federation. Although the Orange Free State was not adverse to such blandishments (especially if they were linked with economic advantage), the Transvaal remained impervious. In 1894 the railway from Johannesburg to Delagoa Bay in Mozambique was opened. Kruger's government grew in wealth and confidence. Perhaps time was not on Rhodes' side after all.

Rhodes' judgement now broke down. His personality had always been a curious one. Squeaky-voiced, never physically robust, obsessed with considerations of hygiene, and abnormally fearful of women, he was by no means the epitome of the masterful empire-builder. Perhaps some of his dormant qualities found their fullest expression in financial wizardry and territorial conquests. Certainly he luxuriated in imperial fantasies. These included the global supremacy of the English-speaking race, the recovery of the United States for the Empire, the extension of British rule throughout Africa, and the populating of Palestine, South America, and the Chinese and Japanese seaboards with British settlers! By 1895 Rhodes aimed at overthrowing Kruger's republic by force.

At first sight this was a not unrealistic aim. The Uitlanders gave assurances that they would rise in rebellion. Rhodes' British South Africa Company could send an armed expedition into the Transvaal from either Rhodesia or Bechuanaland. International indignation would be powerless to prevent the coup. Rhodes himself was Prime Minister of the Cape; Natal would support him. It would be possible to claim that intervention was designed to guarantee the Uitlanders their birth-right of free and equal citizenship.

What part, however, could the British government be expected to play? Even here the time was propitious. The Unionists had won the general election of 1895, and the new Colonial Secretary, Joseph Chamberlain, believed passionately in the need to unify South Africa under British supervision. Even so, Chamberlain's hands were tied by the need to observe certain proprieties. Blatant interference was not possible. It is, however, almost certain that as a result of communications between Rhodes' agent, Harris, and the Colonial Secretary, the latter made plain his overall sympathy for the enterprise. Undoubtedly a successful outcome would have been eagerly appropriated by Chamberlain to further his policies.

But the outcome of the Jameson Raid of 1895–6 was catastrophic. Bad co-ordination between Rhodes and his lieutenant and close friend Dr Jameson, led to an impatient invasion of the Transvaal from Bechuanaland on 31 December 1895. The Uitlander rebellion was a fiasco. Although some revolutionary committees went into action, the majority of Uitlanders remained inert. It was perhaps difficult to expect a prosperous community to man the barricades. Jameson's band was speedily captured by the Transvaalers and handed over to the British authorities for retribution.

'The Hellish Twelve Squad' prepare for the Uitlander rising, planned to coordinate with the Jameson Raid of 1895–6. In the event, the English-speaking citizens of Johannesburg were ineffective rebels.

Homeward bound! Stalwarts of the Jameson Raid sail for England after the fiasco of their enterprise. Dr Jameson (fourth from left) peeps over a companion's shoulder.

Sir Alfred Milner,
Governor of the Cape
(1897–1905). Together
with Chamberlain,
Milner was one of the
chief architects of the
South African War.

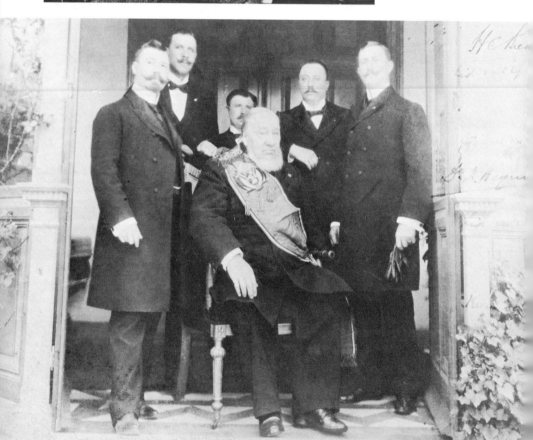

Although Rhodes tried to play down the disaster, he had suffered a prodigious reverse. He was forced to resign as Prime Minister of the Cape, his alliance with Hofmeyer in ruins. Moderate Afrikaner opinion in the Transvaal was swamped by a resurgence of support for Kruger. The Kaiser sent Oom Paul a telegram ringing with congratulation. In Britain, liberal opinion was horrified at the aggression and an inquiry was called for. The official inquiry was handled (or mishandled) by a Commons Committee. An unrepentant Rhodes treated it with insolence. Chamberlain gave nothing away. Complaints were made that even the Liberal members of the Committee were anxious to reveal nothing unpleasant. Certainly the inquiry had every appearance of an exercise in white-washing.

British policy in South Africa now needed restructuring. Accordingly Chamberlain in London, and (after 1897) Alfred Milner, as Governor of the Cape and High Commissioner, set to work. The Transvaal was cut off from outside assistance. In 1898 Germany was bought off with an agreement over the possible future disposal of Portugal's African colonies. In the not unlikely event of Portuguese bankruptcy and collapse, and the subsequent surrender of her colonies, Britain was to have Mozambique and Germany was to have Angola. In September 1898, Arthur Balfour told the Cabinet that Germany had resigned 'all concern in Transvaal matters'. Only two years had elapsed from the Kaiser's enthusiastic telegram to this surrender. No other nation was likely to assist the Transvaal.

Although morally impoverished by the Jameson Raid, Chamberlain, with Milner's assistance, gradually re-established the propaganda campaign on behalf of the Uitlanders. Despite some concessions by Kruger, it was still possible to present them as a worthy group languishing for civil rights. By no means all of Chamberlain's colleagues saw the problem in this light. Salisbury, Balfour, and Hicks Beach (the Chancellor) were acutely aware of the shortcomings in the Uitlander case. Balfour indeed thought the Uitlanders 'rather unreasonable', and argued in a Cabinet paper that 'were I a Boer . . . nothing but necessity would induce me to adopt a constitution which would turn my country into an English Republic, or a system of education that would

In exile. Paul Kruger (wearing the sash of the Transvaal) and his personal staff at Hilversum in the Netherlands, August 1901, while British troops were completing the conquest of his republic. Kruger died in Switzerland in 1904.

reduce my language to the "patois" of a small and helpless minority'.

By 1899, however, events were moving towards a major crisis. In May, a face to face confrontation at Bloemfontein between Kruger and Milner predictably failed to resolve their differences. A month later, Chamberlain and Milner discussed both the form of an ultimatum to the Transvaal and the question of troop reinforcements. In July Kruger announced that he would grant the Uitlanders a seven year retrospective franchise and five new seats in the Volksraad. This diversion brought him little respite. By August it is evident that Chamberlain and Milner were actively preparing for war. The Sudan campaign was conveniently over, and public attention could be focussed on the Transvaal. Several weeks before the outbreak of hostilities in October, nearly 70,000 British troops were either in South Africa or on the high seas.

On 9 October 1899, the British diplomatic offensive was concluded neatly when both the Transvaal and the Orange Free State presented an ultimatum calling for the withdrawal of British troops from the Transvaal's frontiers and the recall of all reinforcements dispatched since June. Since Britain had provoked the ultimatum, it was naturally ignored. Having convinced itself that it was necessary to fight for supremacy in South Africa, the government swallowed its qualms and went ahead.

Boer troops at the siege of Mafeking, 1900. The vast bulk of the Boer army consisted of civilian volunteers who nonetheless handled their modern weaponry with great efficiency.

Optimistic assumptions that the war would soon be over were to be ludicrously inaccurate.

The South African War of 1899–1902 presented the bizarre spectacle of 448,000 men of the British Empire struggling for three years to overcome a largely amateur army of 45,000 Afrikaners. Although eventually victorious, Britain underwent an experience every bit as traumatic as was defeat for the Boer republics. Initially the British army was saddled with incompetent leadership and inadequate preparation. Even when the fumbling Commander-in-Chief Buller had been superseded in December 1899 by the illustrious Roberts and the ruthlessly successful Kitchener, the war still had two and a half years to run. In the end it was sheer weight of numbers and inexhaustible supplies of equipment and munitions that dragged the Afrikaners to defeat.

The war was divided into three distinct phases. Phase one ran from the outbreak of hostilities to the arrival of Roberts and Kitchener in January 1900. It was a period of unprecedented British reverses, beginning with the sieges of the strategically significant towns of Kimberley, Mafeking and Ladysmith. In December, during one 'black week', substantial British armies were repulsed at Stormberg, Magersfontein, and Colenso. These disasters were brought about by a combination of British ineptitude and the brilliantly unorthodox and deter-

Imperial counter-attack. Canadian troops prepare to storm a *kopje* (small hill). The self-governing colonies sent over 55,000 troops to aid Britain in the South African War.

mined tactics of the Boers. Doubtless the extremely efficient modern weaponry purchased with the Transvaal's proceeds from the Rand had its effect. These military humiliations were rapturously observed by bitterly hostile critics of British policy on the continent of Europe.

The second stage of the war was a contrapuntal episode. British forces, marshalled by Roberts and Kitchener, and boasting dashing commanders like John French, swept into the Transvaal and the Free State. Pretoria fell, and the remnants of Kruger's government sped down the railway line to Delagoa Bay. By December 1900 the war seemed as good as over. The Boers had been formally defeated at Paardeberg. Kimberley, Ladysmith and Mafeking had been relieved (the latter to the accompaniment of hysterical rejoicing in London). Although several thousand Cape Dutch had joined the Boer armies, the colony was not torn by civil war. The angry splutterings of European nations were of no use to the two republics. The self-governing colonies had stood firmly behind the British cause and had sent 55,000 men to support it.

Towards the end of 1900 there seemed every reason to suppose that the war would very soon be over. Roberts returned to England, leaving Kitchener in command. Victory parades were held in London. In October the Unionists fought the 'Khaki' election, hoping to capitalise on the apparent triumph in South Africa. The election campaign aroused the bitterest sentiments and was marked by virulent attacks on Chamberlain as the architect of the war. Although the electorate returned the Unionists with a slightly increased majority, it was pointed out that for every eight votes cast for the government, seven were cast against it.

Still, with the war now in its third and longest stage, the government had a mandate for pushing on to the end. The inexorable progress towards final victory was, however, enervating and ugly. The main problem for the British forces lay in tracking down the 15,000 or so Boer commandos still in the field. Led by such gifted generals as Louis Botha, Jan Smuts, Hertzog, de Wet and de la Rey, the commandos made expert use of the terrain and were supplied by the friendly local populace. Strung out over hundreds of miles of veld, the huge

Louis Botha (1862–1919), one of the most gifted of the Boer commanders. Botha contributed equally to reconciliation after the War, and in 1910 became first Prime Minister of the Union of South Africa.

Suntanned and be-
whiskered men of the
Hampshire Regiment,
their column stretching
over the horizon, crossing
the Valsch River Drift
before marching on
Kroonstadt in the Orange
Free State.

Searching for arms in
Pretoria, 1900. The prob-
lem of denying equipment
and supplies to the Boer
commandos still in the
field haunted the British
authorities.

British army now applied controversial counter-measures.

Farm-burning was one means of denying the commandos essential supplies. It went ahead on a massive scale. Between June and November 1900 over 600 farms were burnt in the Orange Free State alone. Naturally this scorched-earth policy made thousands homeless. Partly to cope with the refugees, partly to keep them under supervision, the British authorities herded them into concentration camps. Early deficiencies in diet and sanitation lead to heavy mortalities among the inmates. By June 1902 about 20,000 had died, most of them women and children. A public outcry in Britain caused a prompt improvement in conditions, but deep disquiet remained. To many Afrikaners it seemed as if the British were trying to exterminate them; to some British statesmen, such as the Liberal leader Campbell-Bannerman, it seemed appropriate to speak of 'methods of barbarism'.

At last, in May 1902, the Peace of Vereeniging was signed between the Boer leaders and the British authorities. Although the Transvaal and the Orange Free State were dragged into the Empire, notable concessions were made to Afrikaner susceptibilities. £3,000,000 was set aside to restore families to their homes and work; interest-free loans were made available for two years; Boer troops, on recognising British sovereignty, could take up their civilian lives again. Most significant of all was the shelving of the enfranchisement of non-Europeans until the Transvaal and Orange Free State

Kitchener's counter-measures to commando mobility. Barbed wire, farm-burning and concentration camps were methods used to contain Boer troop movements.

were once more self-governing. In effect, this guaranteed that in these two provinces non-Europeans would remain voteless and underprivileged. The war was over, but the peace threatened to be just as difficult to win.

The South African War provided a water-shed in the development of the Empire. The campaign had proved that imperial expansion was not necessarily glorious or cheap. Various unsavoury episodes had shocked Victorian sensibilities. In England the pro-Boers, Harcourt, Morley, John Burns and the young Lloyd George, had sometimes risked life and limb in their attacks on British policy. Hostile criticism from Europe and the United States heightened British awareness of isolation. After a *fin de siècle* diversion into the cruder excesses of jingoistic imperialism, the British returned with a proper sense of guilt to nobler purposes.

In yet another sense the war had been instructive. As Kipling ruefully admitted:

> Let us admit it fairly, as a business people should.
> We have had no end of a lesson: it will do us no
> end of good.

The evident inadequacies of British arms prompted an avalanche of reform. The Committee of Imperial Defence was established. The Elgin Commission, and the War Office (Reconstitution) Committee, recommended sweeping reforms. Between 1902 and 1904 Britain concluded an alliance with Japan, and the entente with France. Britain thus emerged from the

Still at large. De Wet's commandos crossing the Orange river.

humiliations of the Boer War in a stronger position than after many previous victories.

In South Africa itself the aftermath of war was perhaps less encouraging. Although in 1903 Alfred Milner had persuaded the four colonies and Rhodesia to join a customs union, the federation of South Africa had not been achieved by the time of his resignation in 1905. In the long run the overall aims of 'Milnerism' failed. Permanent British supremacy was not established in South Africa; the wider use of English did not relegate Afrikaans to the status of a second class language; Afrikaner nationalism was not swamped by the rising tide of Anglo-Saxon cultural influence and constitutional practice. Indeed it is arguable that the war refined and subtly strengthened Afrikaner nationalism, making it much more difficult to browbeat and subvert.

To be sure, British control of the Rand's industries was now guaranteed. In the Transvaal the English-speaking Uitlanders became full citizens, thus fulfilling the alleged chief objective of the war. The regulations applying to African workers (especially the miners) were certainly improved and liberalised. A somewhat more humanitarian approach characterised the official attitude towards the non-Europeans. The Simonstown naval base could expect decades of security. All this had changed.

But when in 1906 the new Liberal government of Campbell-Bannerman gave the Transvaal and the

Afrikaner women washing clothes at Springfontein concentration camp. The high mortality rate in the concentration camps was the result of poor organisation rather than British malevolence. After a public outcry, conditions were drastically improved, but meanwhile about 20,000 inmates had perished.

Bringing him home! The South African War ended in May 1902, but the newly conquered territories provided Chamberlain and his successors at the Colonial Office with a good many fresh problems.

Orange Free State their autonomy, there were complaints in Britain that the fruits of victory had been cast away. The first responsible government of the Transvaal was headed by Botha and Smuts of the recently formed Het Volk party. In the 1907 election Afrikaner solidarity had triumphed over the divided political allegiance of the English-speaking Transvaalers. The Uitlanders were apparently as unreliable in victory as they had previously been in adversity.

As it happened, the victory of Het Volk brought benefits to British interests. Botha and Smuts were Afrikaner leaders of broader vision and more urbane sympathies than the departed Krugerite hierarchy. The old alliance between Afrikaner moderates and English-speaking South Africans was revived within a wider political framework. This alliance dominated the first years of the Union of South Africa after 1910, and in 1914 the two ex-commando generals, Botha and Smuts, led their people into the Great War on Britain's side. Although this would have greatly satisfied Cecil Rhodes and Joseph Chamberlain, it did not exactly conform to their previous calculations.

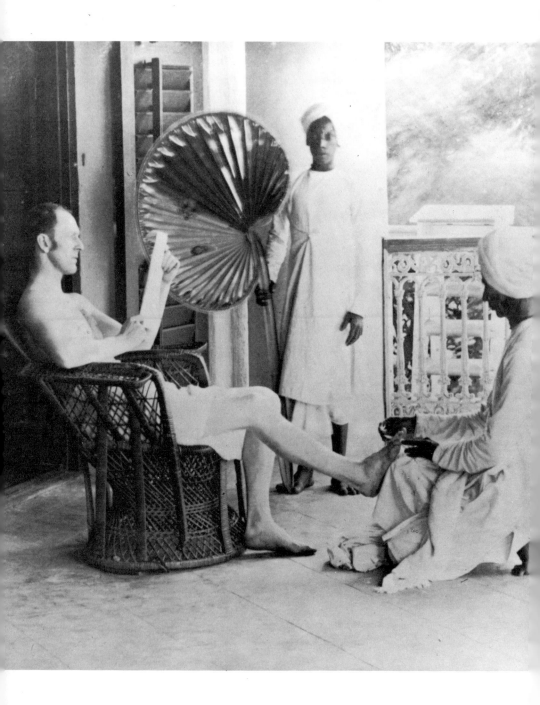

9   The Raj in India 1870-1905

*Conservative and Liberal interpretations of the Raj, 1870–84;
Second Afghan War; Lord Ripon and reform; establishment
of Indian National Congress 1885; India's value to Britain;
sahibs, memsahibs, and babus; the Viceregal office. The Curzon
era: India at the end of the century; Curzon's aims as Viceroy;
domestic and frontier policies; the quarrel with Kitchener, and
Curzon's resignation.*

BETWEEN 1869 and 1880 Conservative governments
selected two Viceroys, Lord Mayo and Lord Lytton,
who stamped their mark on India. Mayo, very much his
own master, did much to insulate the office from party
pressures, for although appointed when Disraeli's administration was in its death throes, he subsequently
appealed to his Conservative friends to support Gladstone's government over Indian affairs. The viceroyalty
of his successor, Northbrook, was somewhat colourless
in comparison and marked by some sharp differences
between the Liberal Viceroy and the Conservative
Secretary of State, Lord Salisbury.

From 1876–80 Lord Lytton ruled at Calcutta.
Especially selected by Disraeli to give vibrant expression to the Raj, Lytton's dashing and ambitious policies
led to disaster and humiliation. Although Mayo had
argued that 'we hold India by a thread', he also insisted
that 'we must gradually associate with ourselves in the
Government of this country more of the native element'.
Lytton also saw the desirability of closer identification
with Indians, but he believed that an alliance with the
princes would best serve British interests. The inert
masses and the potentially troublesome 'babus' (educated Indians) could not be relied upon. These convictions were given formal approval when Disraeli made
Queen Victoria Empress of India in 1876. The loyalist
Indian princes could now identify more closely than

Benefits of the Raj.
Service in India not only
demanded high-minded
administration, but
usually carried high
salaries and numerous
other advantages.

165

ever before with a fellow-ruler who also represented the paramount power in the sub-continent.

But in England the Liberal party launched a campaign against the Bill making Victoria Empress, and followed this up by attacking the fundamentals of Conservative policy towards India. Gladstone reasserted some of the moral implications of British rule first picked out by Pitt's India Act a century before. The Liberals contended that essentially India should be governed for the good of the Indians. They accordingly opposed the restrictions on native-language newspapers imposed by the Act of 1878, and pressed for the admission of more Indians to the higher reaches of the Civil Service. The logical extension of these policies was that Indians should gradually assume a greater share in their own government; perhaps one day even become self-governing.

The last period of Lytton's viceroyalty ended in circumstances guaranteed to give pleasure to Liberal critics. Convinced that Russia was gaining undue influence over Afghanistan, Lytton cajoled and hoodwinked the Cabinet into authorising an invasion. The

Below: Uneasy occupation. Officers of the Royal Artillery in Kabul, 1879–80.

First right: Lord Lytton, Conservative Viceroy (1876–80).
Second right: Lord Ripon, Liberal Viceroy (1880–4).

early success of the enterprise was striking, and a treaty was signed by which the new Amir promised to support British foreign policy and receive a British Resident at Kabul. Certain border districts and the Khyber and Mishmi Passes were placed under British control. In return, Britain guaranteed the Amir military aid against foreign aggression (an ironical item) and undertook an annual subsidy of six lakhs of rupees.

This agreeable state of affairs was short-lived. In September 1879 the British Resident was murdered by Afghan soldiers. As a counter-measure British forces occupied Kabul, causing the accommodating Amir Yakub to abdicate. Britain now had to decide how much of Afghanistan she was going to control and who she planned to put on the throne in place of Yakub. Before any definite outcome had been achieved, however, the Conservatives were heavily defeated in the general election of 1880.

The incoming Liberal administration had been fiercely critical of Lytton's Afghan policy while in Opposition.

Once in power their antagonism became tempered with more practical considerations. The new Viceroy, Lord Ripon, toyed with the idea of maintaining control of at least some of the border land, and General Roberts fought a successful campaign to maintain the British-backed Amir, Abdur Rahman, against the rebellious Ayub, brother of the deposed Amir Yakub. Gladstone then withdrew all British troops from Afghanistan, and Lytton's policy of forcibly excluding Russian influence from Afghanistan was replaced by attempts to reach an understanding with St Petersburg instead. Fears of Russian intentions, however, despite the frequently unrealistic nature of such fears, remained uppermost in the minds of defence strategists.

Ripon's viceroyalty (1880–4) was marked by significant reforms in India. The restrictive Press Act was repealed, and Indian newspapers allowed to publish subject only to the limitations of libel and sedition. More important still was Ripon's attempt to give more power to local representative institutions such as municipal and provincial councils. This was certainly in accord with Gladstone's hope, expressed in 1883, that the Commons would press ahead with the 'noble and upright and blessed work of gradually increasing the Indian franchise'.

These laudably progressive sentiments provoked stiff opposition from the British community in India and from Conservatives at home. Even some Liberals were now convinced that Gladstone, already the apostle of Irish Home Rule, meant to supervise the dissolution of the Empire. Critics of Liberal policy claimed, with some justice, that the Indian masses wanted good government, not the vote, and saw anarchy, bloodshed and ruin at the end of the path marked out by the reformers. The Liberal initiative of 1880–5 was therefore stamped out by the return of the Conservatives to power in 1886.

Apart from a break between 1892 and 1895, the Unionist party (that alliance of Conservatives, Liberal Unionists, and Chamberlainite Radicals born out of the Home Rule crisis of 1885–6) ruled from 1886 to 1905. These years saw the last major annexation of territory in Asia when Lord Salisbury's government, fearful of French influence, conquered Upper Burma. This meant that the whole of Burma was now made a province of

Right: British order in Mandalay. Burmese street sweepers marching to work, 1886.

Below: The Indian army was maintained out of Indian revenue. In this *Punch* cartoon of 1896: *India* complains: 'I have found the men, sahib. Why should I find the money *too*?' *John Bull:* ''Pon my word, my dear. I really don't see why you should.'

the Indian Empire. Until the beginning of Lord Curzon's viceroyalty (1898–1905), the Raj did not distinguish itself by its reforms. An Indian Councils Act was passed in 1892 with the support of the Liberal Opposition, but its extension of representation and its encouragement of freer discussions on the provincial councils did not greatly advance Indian self-determination.

A more significant pointer to the future lay in the establishment of the Indian National Congress in 1885. Far from being the irresistible product of Indian nationalism, Congress was considered an appropriate safety valve by the administration. If educated Indians could rid themselves of pent-up grievances through participating in annual conferences of this sort, the Raj would be well pleased. Perhaps an organisation like the Congress was all the more necessary after the recent fiasco of the Ilbert Bill. This measure of legal reform had proposed that Indian magistrates should be allowed to try Europeans brought before the courts. The almost

unanimous outcry from the British community in India
had led to the drastic amendment of the Bill. To many
educated Indians this surrender was further evidence
that there was an enormous gap between the theory and
the practice of the government.

The main reason for the erratic nature of reform in
India was quite simply that Britain could not afford to
lose her greatest dependency. About one-fifth of the
total British investment overseas was sunk in India; a
sum of between £270,000,000 and £300,000,000 by the

THE INDIAN LADIES' MAGAZINE

Vol. I.]   **AUGUST, 1901.**   [No. 2.

CONTENTS.

	PAGE
Ourselves	25
Queen Victoria and Queen Alexandra.—(Illustrated)	26
Social Intercourse between European and Indian Ladies	29
Col. Meadows Taylor's "Seeta": A Study	31
The Vedic Wife	34
In the Forest:—A Poem	36
"A Little Child shall lead them":—A Hindu Story	37
Pundita Ramabai and her Work.—(Illustrated)	40
Miss Marie Corelli on "Sovran Woman"	43
Friendly Chats between Ourselves:—The Home	45
Seriousness: A Fancy	46
The Low-Caste Wife: A Sketch from Life	48
An Indian Lady's Appreciation	49
Editorial Notes:—Women's Work in the Handicrafts; Miss Ghosal on the Education of Indian Girls	50
Things Seen:—The Marina	52
Indian Cookery	52
Correspondence:—Lady Ampthill's Women's Memorial to Queen Victoria.; The Maharani's Girls' College, Mysore; A Famous Indian Lady	53
News and Notes	55

end of the century. India took nineteen per cent of British exports. The Indian army was a readily available source of manpower which did not cost the British taxpayer one penny. Indeed the whole administration of the Raj, let alone the army, was financed by taxes levied on the Indian people. Although it was possible to boast that India had never been so well governed, the fact was that Indians not only paid for their own government but had no say in its structure.

In some ways the Raj was a bluff. 300,000,000 Indians were ruled by barely 1,500 administrators of the Indian Civil Service. There were perhaps 3,000 British officers in the Indian army. Leaving aside the British regiments serving in India, the total number of Britons in India at the end of Victoria's reign was something like 20,000. If the Indian people had chosen to throw off their overlords there would have been little to prevent them. The scarlet-coated infantry tramping down the Grand Trunk Road, the double firsts of the Indian Civil Service, the social exclusiveness of the British clubs, the temperate justice of the English Common Law, would have been of no avail. High-minded administration could not have withstood a united and vengeful people.

Fortunately for the British, there was no prospect of such unanimity in the 1890's. The overwhelming majority of the educated Indian élite wished to influence the Raj through reasoned argument and constitutional pressures. The Indian masses, struggling for subsistence, had no time to entertain seditious thoughts. In village India the tempo of life had hardly changed since the days of the Emperors Akhbar and Aurangzeb. In the towns it was to be some years yet before factory workers and mill hands became radical and socialist agitators. Princely India (some quarter of the whole) was reliably conservative.

Paradoxically, both the inertia of the masses and the growing assertiveness of educated Indians confirmed the bulk of the British administrators, businessmen, and soldiers in India in their conviction that the Raj must be preserved. The educated babus must be put firmly in their place. Lord Lytton argued that 'the encouragement of natives does not mean the supremacy of Baboodom', and even the Liberal Viceroy Dufferin (1884-8) announced that 'the Bengali Baboo is a most

Symbol of emancipation, *The Indian Ladies Magazine* was enlightened for the times.

troublesome and irritating gentleman . . . we must not show ourselves at all afraid of him'. As for Indians in general, the comfortable assertion of British supremacy found ample official backing in pronouncements like that of the Viceroy Lord Mayo when he said 'we are all British gentlemen engaged in the magnificent work of governing an inferior race'.

Ignoring the embarrassing excellence of India's ancient culture, and insisting (if pressed) that although most Indians were members of the Aryan race they belonged to the most backward sub-section, the British in India continued to live self-contained and confident lives. The inconsiderate intensity of the climate, the unpredictable outbreaks of contagion, the dirt and squalor of native India, could all be kept at bay. To this end, British communities lived in separate cantonments, and sent their children to English public schools, or to Indian schools modelled faithfully, if a trifle absurdly, on the rigorous establishments back home.

The thousands of British children who were, over the years, born in India could therefore live from the cradle to the grave in a simulated Englishness set in an oriental sub-continent. Bacon and eggs for breakfast, lamb and redcurrant jelly for dinner, all cooked and served by brown hands. Indian ayahs staffed the nurseries, and sang 'Baa Baa Black Sheep' in Hindi accents. To escape from the stifling summers on the plains, women and children were often packed off to hill stations where the air was crisp and cholera usually at a safe distance. The most famous retreat of all was Simla.

Simla was, for half the year, the capital of the Indian Empire. The Viceroy, his advisers, and his minions took themselves off to grapple with the Raj's problems in the invigorating air of the Himalayan foot-hills. Simla was a higgledy-piggledy place, with Anglican church towers next to Indian-Gothic next to administrative utilitarian. The paths were steep and narrow, and carriages generally banned. With its vigorous social life and its holiday atmosphere, Simla must have seemed like a ridiculously well-patronised ski resort – without the skiing.

Indian ayah and young charge.

The magnificence of the viceregal office could not only be glimpsed at Simla. In Calcutta, and later at New Delhi, the Viceroy lived like an Emperor. Of course, he *was* an Emperor – by proxy at least. His

Multi-racial group. Social mixing between British and Indians, though often uneasy, was by no means unknown.

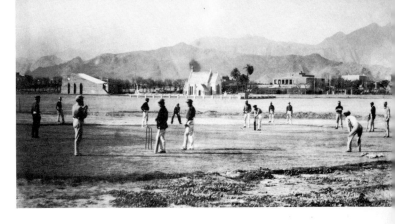

One of Britain's most successful exports. A cricket match in 1896.

palace at Calcutta contained a labyrinth of corridors and stately rooms guarded by towering, bearded Sikhs. He was, by calculation and circumstance, one of the least accessible rulers in the world. The Caesars had been open to public petition, it was quite in order to write a humble note to Queen Victoria, but to contact the Viceroy one had first to approach the right department of the Indian Civil Service. On many state occasions, the Viceroy was merely a remote figure swaying on the back of a bejewelled elephant (which was itself surrounded by other gorgeously apparelled beasts) making one small item in an endless flow of bright uniforms, flashing lances, and brass bands.

For all the pomp and splendour, it was by no means easy to fill the position of Viceroy. Those whom the government wished to appoint were often reluctant to serve, and many of those who clamoured for the job were downright unsuitable. If taken seriously, a term as Viceroy involved backbreaking toil and staggering responsibilities. On the other hand, it put the incumbent on well-nigh equal terms with the Emperor of China for four or five years. To a certain extent, the Viceroy was also his own master. Provided that he could carry his Executive Council (virtually his Cabinet) with him, there were many areas in which he could exercise considerable initiative. The great departments of the Indian Civil Service were his to galvanise or neglect. Internal improvements, trade, defence (which was often an exercise in foreign policy) could become fields of intense activity. Provided the Viceroy avoided a head-on clash with the British government, the outlet for his enterprise was unlimited.

The Viceroy's office attained something of an apotheosis under Lord Curzon. From 1898 to 1905 Curzon's boundless energy and reforming zeal were unleashed upon India. If the highest ranks of the Indian Civil Service were filled by the heaven born, the viceroyalty

View of Simla, with its bizarre mixture of architectural styles.

Lord Curzon, Viceroy 1898–1905. Curzon typified the assurance, incorruptibility and arrogance of the Raj at its zenith.

Below: Curzon rides in state at the Delhi durbar of 1903.

was now occupied (not least in the opinion of the incumbent himself) by the Almighty. It must have seemed no coincidence to Curzon that the viceregal palace at Calcutta was modelled on his ancestral home, Kedleston Hall in Derbyshire. He had an extraordinarily high opinion of his abilities, and the vast sub-continent seemed an appropriate place to exercise his gifts.

In some measure, Curzon's self-confidence was quite justifiable, and his claims to superiority based on real achievement. He became Viceroy at the age of thirty-eight, after a brilliant career in the Conservative party had brought him early to the Parliamentary Under-Secretaryships of both the Foreign and India Offices. In the meantime he had married one of the apparently endless supply of nubile daughters of American millionaires, and had also travelled widely in Asia. Before his appointment as Viceroy he had written three books based on his journeys, and had come to the conclusion that the continuing mastery of India was the keystone to Britain's imperial status. Curzon gave typically dramatic expression to this conviction when he said, 'As long as we rule India we are the greatest power in the world. If we lose it, we shall drop straightaway to a third-rate power'.

But for all Curzon's vigour and inspiration, his character was flawed, his personality abrasive. His pride and condescension were infuriating qualities. Few

Famine victims, 1900. India provided absurd contrasts between opulence and destitution. In the great famine of 1900 it was estimated that between ten and fifteen million people died.

colleagues were able to live up to his rigorous standards, or to escape his impatience and contempt. His incorruptibility was in part founded on self-regard, and his insistence that justice must be done to Indians was based on the philosophy that the British could only hold India by proving themselves impartial and high-minded administrators. It is also arguable that his impartiality sprang from his low regard for mankind in general. Despising both the lower orders in Britain and the Indian masses, Curzon saw no reason why both should not be given good government from above.

In a way, Curzon's reforms in India marked not the beginning of a new era but the dazzling end of an old one. Although sensitive to the point of paranoia over his own position, Curzon was curiously insensitive to the susceptibilities of others. He regarded Indians as

An untouchable.
This sweeper girl was one
of the millions of Indian
untouchables. The Raj
did little to improve their
position.

morally inferior to Englishmen and took little trouble
to disguise his opinions. In 1901 he informed Arthur
Balfour that the real strength of his position lay in 'the
extraordinary inferiority, in character, honesty and
capacity of the [Indians]. It is often said why not make
some prominent native a member of the Executive
Council? The answer is that in the whole continent
there is not an Indian fit for the post.' Thus Curzon's
vision of India was narrowly confined to the awe-
inspiring and stately progress of the Raj. He set aside
the rising aspirations of Indian nationalism with a short-
sightedness that now seems positively perverse. Perhaps,
in this respect, Curzon could only see what he wanted
to see.

The complexities of governing India, however, were
plain enough. First there was the daunting size of the

country. At the end of Victoria's reign the Indian Empire comprised some 12,000 square miles more than Europe, without Russia. The population was nearly 300,000,000, of whom over a quarter lived in princely India. This total was one-fifth of mankind. Hinduism was the religion of seventy per cent of the Indian people, Islam the faith of twenty-one per cent. In 1901 less than nine per cent of the population of British India was employed in industry, and roughly seventy per cent were completely dependent upon agriculture. This lack of economic diversity, coupled with a steady population increase, meant that famines periodically swept India, causing millions to starve to death.

The economic needs of Britain had held back Indian industry. With no fiscal autonomy in the nineteenth century, India had been forced to play the dual role of provider of raw materials and market for British manufactures. The Indian cotton industry had been blatantly manipulated for the benefit of Lancashire. Despite this there were nearly two hundred cotton mills in India by the turn of the century, and the jute and tea industries were profitable enterprises. Heavy industry had still to develop, but the sinews of growth (docks, railways, roads) were already there in some measure. The Indian education system, however, was ill-designed to produce scientists and technologists. Less than one-fifth of boys

Baluchi chieftains, 1877. The Baluchis were proud and warlike tribesmen on the north-west frontier.

The Raj as policeman. Dictating terms to north-west frontiersmen, 1896.

attended primary school, and only one girl out of forty. By 1901 the five universities had high failure rates, and were chiefly geared to the production of graduates to serve some branches of the administration.

At the end of the nineteenth century, therefore, India was still overwhelmingly agricultural, illiterate, fatalistic, and backward. Curzon did not aspire to drag the Indian people into the twentieth century. He was, however, determined to enforce governmental efficiency, and to purify and reinforce the administration. He incidentally forced through reforms which were bound to better Indian conditions. Thus a new famine policy was established by 1903. The railway system was improved. Farmers were given better credit facilities, and government-sponsored research into agriculture begun. Plans were laid for extending the irrigation system, and an attempt was made to improve Indian education at both school and university level.

More controversial was Curzon's campaign to ensure Indians justice in cases involving Europeans. In particular, the Viceroy came down heavily on outrages committed by the army. In 1899 he insisted on the due punishment of soldiers of the Royal West Kent Regiment for the particularly brutal rape of a Burmese woman. In April 1902 he secured the punishment of every man of the Ninth Lancers, after two soldiers had beaten an Indian cook to death. Given the past practice of the military courts to play down such incidents, Curzon's vengeful intervention was a valuable innovation. Although it brought him the hatred of a large part

179

of the army, his attitude was warmly welcomed by the Indian press. Indeed, it is possible to see this support precisely in the terms of Curzon's bid to convince the Indians that British rule was juster and purer than any other rule could be.

Curzon's frontier policy was conducted with the same single-mindedness as his domestic reforms. Unfortunately for him it brought him into sharp conflict with the British government. This confrontation was due partly to a fundamental disagreement over the basis of Curzon's policy and partly over the methods he used to pursue this policy. Basically, Curzon and the Balfour government disagreed over the extent of the Russian menace on the frontiers of India. Balfour was convinced by 1904 that Russian policy no longer included plans for an invasion of India, and he dismissed past fears of such an invasion as 'a scare . . . of the most foolish description'.

There were good reasons for playing down the Russian threat. The Anglo-Japanese alliance of 1902 provided the British Empire in Asia with strong support – as evidenced in the speedy defeat of Russia in the Russo-Japanese War of 1904–5. The entente with France was yet another promising development, for France had been Russia's ally since 1894. In addition the British government succeeded in 1904 in coming to an agreement with Russia over their mutual interests in Indian border states like Tibet and Afghanistan. Both sides promised to practice non-intervention.

But non-intervention was anathema to Curzon. He was obsessed by Russian expansion in Asia. In the 1890's he had pressed for the establishment of British naval supremacy in the Persian Gulf and had advocated the extension of British influence in southern Persia. Now, as Viceroy, he was determined to exclude Russia from both Afghanistan and Tibet. Both he and the British government could agree that the Russian presence put diplomatic pressure on Britain both in Asia and in Europe. But Curzon tended to see Russian interference where none existed, and to advocate violent counter-strokes rather than diplomatic overtures.

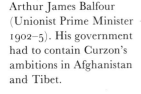

Punitive expedition. A mounted battery in action 1895.

Thus Curzon wished to bind the Amir Habibulla of Afghanistan to support British policy under a formal and exacting treaty. In particular, the Viceroy wanted the Indian army to have the right to enter Afghanistan if Russia invaded. The British government, however, preferred to continue with the more comfortable arrangement that Britain would merely act as a guarantor of Afghan independence. An agreement on these lines was concluded in 1905. Curzon was incensed, and derided the 'Afghan surrender' as the work of a 'moribund government with fear of Russia on the brain'. Although the Cabinet had certainly displayed caution, this was preferable to rash undertakings.

Arthur James Balfour (Unionist Prime Minister 1902–5). His government had to contain Curzon's ambitions in Afghanistan and Tibet.

Curzon's Tibetan policy was equally headstrong. Convinced that Russian influence was growing in Tibet, Curzon planned a mission to assert British interests. The project was beset with difficulties. To begin with, Tibet was technically under the suzerainty of China, which was in itself a complicating factor. In addition, what exactly was the mission to accomplish? The British government was vehemently opposed to any permanent entanglement. Curzon, on the other hand, wanted to extract long-term military and political concessions from the Tibetans. Although the Cabinet eventually gave the Viceroy grudging permission to launch a limited expedition, Curzon hoped to present them with a brilliant fait accompli that would sweep away their reservations. The 'man on the spot' would have exceeded his instructions, but won his case.

By December 1903 the Tibetan expedition was on the move. It was commanded by Colonel Younghusband, a celebrated explorer and a dedicated mystic. The true nature of the mission was soon revealed. In March and May 1904 there were bloody encounters with Tibetan forces, several hundred of whom were mown down with maxim guns. Younghusband pressed on to the forbidden city of Lhasa, and there negotiated a treaty with the Tibetan leaders. The commercial terms of this treaty were uncontroversial and innocuous. More explosive was the provision for British forces to occupy the strategically important Chumbi valley against an indemnity payable over seventy-five years.

This precipitated a head-on clash between Curzon and the British Cabinet. The latter insisted that Younghusband had been instructed to impose only a three year indemnity. Younghusband subsequently claimed that these instructions had arrived too late to be included in the treaty. Balfour, sure that Younghusband had disobeyed his orders, vetoed the original treaty, and the milder provisions favoured by the government were implemented. The whole episode was thus another humiliation, and a deserved one, for Curzon. The British and Indian governments had clearly not acted in accord, and the resulting confusion gave substance to Balfour's ironic judgement that Curzon's unbridled policy 'would raise India to the position of an independent and not always friendly power'.

Curzon's last years as Viceroy were occupied with an even greater clash of wills. In October 1902, Kitchener, the nation's hero, conqueror of dervishes and Boers, left England to take up his appointment as Commander-in-Chief of the Indian army. A major conflict between the imperious Viceroy and the autocratically inclined Commander-in-Chief was likely from the first, despite Curzon's initial optimism that they would together carry through striking reforms. A bitter quarrel in fact developed over Kitchener's desire to abolish the Military Member of the Viceroy's Council. This permanent official supervised military spending and supply. Kitchener's determination to scrap this post was perhaps strengthened by the fact that the Military Member, Major-General Elles, was an efficient and ambitious officer who guarded his powers jealously.

Celebrations of the Raj. Indian crowds milling before a statue of Queen Victoria at the Delhi Durbar, 1903.

Curzon, eloquent and alarmist, defended the office on the grounds it prevented the Commander-in-Chief from exercising autocratic control. Kitchener, mute and unmovable, stuck to his guns. To the accompaniment of persistent and histrionic viceregal protests, the quarrel dragged on until May 1905. Finally the British government, unwilling to cast down Kitchener and anxious for a united front in India, overrode Curzon's protests. After struggling for some months to side-step this decision, the Viceroy resigned in August, 1905.

As Curzon left India, the reverberations of the quarrel with Kitchener were matched by the outcry over the 1905 partition of Bengal. Although there was much to be said for partition on administrative grounds, it had ignored Bengali tradition and sensibilities. The Indian Congress, which Curzon had dismissed in 1900 as 'tottering to its fall', took up the clamour. More radical voices were heard demanding Indian independence. An unprecedented display of militant nationalism marked Curzon's departure from the country which he had hoped to bind even closer to the British Empire.

This was the final irony of Curzon's viceroyalty. In the last resort, those reforms that had been masterfully introduced failed to satisfy new Indian aspirations. Curzon had played the game brilliantly, but according to rules that were already out of date. His successors had to grapple with problems which he had refused to recognise. Although Curzon had planned to prolong the Raj indefinitely, its collapse was barely forty years away.

10 Egypt and the Sudan

The Khedive's financial problems; Disraeli purchases the Khedive's shares; Anglo-French Dual Control; growing resentments, and Arabi's revolt; the British invasion of 1882; Cromer and reform; the British presence in Egypt; the Mahdi and the Sudan; Gordon at Khartoum; the reaction to his death; Kitchener's reconquest; Omdurman, and the Fashoda Incident; the Anglo-Egyptian condominium.

THE OPENING of the Suez Canal brought no immediate benefits either to the Khedive or to the Egyptian people. Indeed, the Canal Company's revenue for the four years after 1869 was disappointingly low. This was chiefly due to an initial reservation on the part of ship-owners over re-routing their vessels. Eventually the amount of freight increased and, by 1874, the Company was able to reward its shareholders suitably, and repay outstanding interest on loans. Talk of liquidation died away, and de Lesseps was able to issue bonds worth 35,000,000 francs.

The fortunes of the Khedive showed no such improvement. In many ways, Ismail's enlightened attempt to develop irrigation, agriculture, and communications brought him more tribulation than joy. These schemes, while commending the Khedive to European opinion, also put him deeper into debt with European creditors. Unable to purge his own administration of corruption, he reeled from financial crisis to financial crisis, and gradually exhausted his credit in London and Paris.

British policy towards Egypt in the 1870's aimed at restoring the Khedive's finances and at cooperating with France in the supervision of Egyptian affairs. Disraeli's purchase of the bankrupt Ismail's shares in the Suez Canal Company in 1875 was not so much a bid for supremacy as an attempt to buy parity with France in the Company. Certainly this episode had the flamboyance of a typical Disraeli coup, culminating in the Prime Minister's message to the Queen: 'It is just

'Mosé in Egitto!!!'
Disraeli negotiates the purchase of the Khedive's Suez Canal shares in 1875.

settled; you have it, Madam. The French government has been out-generalled'. There was also the unorthodox and rather attractive manner in which the purchase had been financed. According to Disraeli's private secretary, Lowry-Corry, Baron de Rothschild was asked to put up the £4,000,000 loan, Rothschild asked, 'When?' Lowry-Corry replied 'Tomorrow'. After eating a grape, the financier said 'What is your security?' 'The British Government', answered Lowry-Corry. 'You shall have it', said Rothschild.

Anglo-French financial involvement in Egypt, in addition to their strategic concerns, was bound to drag them into further interference in Egypt's domestic concerns. In May 1876 Ismail, unable to maintain his repayments of interest, had to accept the establishment of an international *Caisse de la Dette Publique* which was to handle his revenues and ensure the appropriate repayments to foreign bankers. French initiative subsequently forced Britain to accept the principle of even greater oversight of Egypt's finances. Thus the era of dual control began. A British and a French controller supervised the Egyptian finance departments.

In 1878 France, backed by Britain, forced the Khedive to appoint a responsible ministry headed by Nubar Pasha, and including one French and one British minister. Ismail's personal revenues and estates were put under the charge of the new ministry. In return for his translation into something like a constitutional monarch, the Khedive received yet another loan. The determination of Britain and France to create solvency out of bankruptcy, however, necessitated an attack on entrenched privileges in Egypt. By 1879 the European overseers had united the army, and much of the old order, against them. Profiting from this situation, Ismail dismissed his European ministers and attempted to dispense with foreign control. Britain and France reacted promptly by getting the Turkish Sultan to depose the Khedive and appoint his son Tewfik in his place.

The deposition of Ismail illustrated the realities of Anglo-French influence, but it naturally did nothing to abate Egyptian resentment. The new Khedive was little more than a European puppet; foreign financial control continued. Both sides were trapped by the perennial

Colonel Arabi. His anti-European rebellion precipitated the British invasion of Egypt in 1882.

crisis of Egyptian indebtedness. Nearly twenty-five per cent of Egypt's revenue went merely to repay interest. Solvency seemed to be possible only under European supervision. Yet Britain in particular would have preferred to have exercised corrective influence from a distance. Unfortunately a precedent of intervention had now been established, and events in Egypt moved swiftly towards another confrontation.

The revolt led by Colonel Arabi came to its climax in 1881. From early 1879 Arabi and the Egyptian army had been foremost among the bitter critics of the continuing European manipulation of the Egyptian administration. Other groups had their resentments too. Liberal reformers joined hands with uneasy landowners and Moslem traditionalists. The long-suffering peasantry had been squeezed dry by Khedival extortions. Although these diverse elements had little in common in normal circumstances, they now shared a dislike of foreign control and wished to end it. The army was fearful of its place in a subordinated Egypt and was prepared to take action to protect its position. Although to speak of a clear-cut nationalist movement would be an exaggeration, there is no doubt that the one bond between these malcontents was anti-European sentiment.

In 1881 Arabi and the colonels wrung a series of concessions from the Khedive Tewfik. In February the Minister for War was dismissed. In September the ministry was forced from office, the army restored to its former strength, and the Chamber of Notables recalled. Tewfik managed, for a time, both to surrender and to convince Britain and France that surrender was not irreparable. When Arabi became Minister for War, however, and one of his supporters Prime Minister, it was plain that the new Egyptian government was going to pursue policies at odds with Anglo-French interests.

Gladstone's Cabinet was now faced with an unpalatable choice. Either they could rely on Arabi's assurances that the Canal would be safe in his hands, or they could forcibly assert British supremacy in Egypt. Gladstone himself had no easy answers. His political principles included a steadfast recognition of British interests and an insistence on moral rectitude in foreign affairs. His colleagues were dangerously divided on the issue. The Liberal-Radicals, Chamberlain, Dilke, Morley, were non-interventionists; the Whigs, Hartington, Northbrook, Kimberley, were for coercion.

For some time the British government took steps short of invasion. A Joint Note was sent from Paris and London urging the Khedive (somewhat improperly) to assert his authority. An Anglo-French naval demonstration off Alexandria sought to overawe Arabi. British officials in Egypt painted a lurid and misleading picture of military dictatorship and widespread anarchy. Then in June 1882 serious rioting in Alexandria resulted in the deaths of about forty Europeans. Contemporary reports were more horrendous in their estimates; one spoke of 300 dead, another of 238. News of the riots, and the accumulation of alarmist official reports on the domestic situation in Egypt, helped to unite the British Cabinet behind intervention.

With a weak French government unwilling to commit itself to further joint military action, and failing to find

The British bombardment of Alexandria, 1882. A knocked-out Egyptian gun.

a satisfactory formula for cooperation with the Turkish Sultan, the British Cabinet instructed Beauchamp Seymour, Admiral of the Fleet at Alexandria, to take further action. Seymour eventually issued an ultimatum demanding that all work on Egyptian forts at Alexandria should cease. Despite a reasonable response from the Egyptian government which invited the Admiral to dismantle three guns from any fort he chose, the ultimatum was at the same time rejected. The Royal Navy then proceeded to bombard Alexandria causing substantial damage.

The Khedive Tewfik hastened to place himself under British protection, and General Wolseley arrived at Alexandria empowered to overthrow Arabi in the Khedive's name. The battle of Tel-el-Kebir resulted in

the rout of the Egyptian army. The British government could claim that it had invaded Egypt to restore the Khedive's authority and to create order out of chaos and subversion. In fact, intervention had been prompted by the need to safeguard the Suez route. Ironically the Canal seems at no time to have been in real danger. Colonal Arabi made no attempt to block the waterway, probably because de Lesseps had extravagantly assured him that no British soldier would set foot in the Canal zone. It is also likely that Arabi was a far more responsible influence than contemporary European opinion would admit. At any rate, the British occupation of Egypt had begun.

There is little doubt that Gladstone did not envisage a permanent British presence in Egypt. Annexation was clearly out of the question. The ideal solution would have been the speedy restoration of the Egyptian finances, and the establishment of a stable administration on good terms with the European powers. Sir Evelyn

After the victory of Tel-el-Kebir, 1882. British troops lean nonchalantly against the Sphinx.

Baring (later Lord Cromer) was sent as Consul-General to effect these desirable reforms. Cromer remained in Egypt from 1883 to 1907, during which time he was the effective ruler – or, at least, he ruled Egypt's rulers. His early assessment of his task soon crushed the optimism of those who counted on a quick withdrawal. Solvency, Cromer announced, would not be achieved overnight. It would be a long haul to cleanse the administration of corruption and balance the budget.

These liberal aims provided a comfortable justification for the exercise of British interests. It was the Canal that had turned the Gladstone Cabinet into aggressors, not the plight of the Egyptian peasantry. But for the significance of the short route to India and the East, it is unlikely that the crumbling Khedivate would have been shored up by British bayonets. Equally it became impossible to envisage Britain abandoning the Canal without guarantees so firm as to be unobtainable. Despite numerous official statements that the British presence was only temporary, it in fact lasted for over seventy years.

An attempt was soon made, however, to allay international misgivings over Britain's role in Egypt. In 1888 the Suez Canal Convention guaranteed all nations freedom of passage through the Canal. Although the Egyptian government was charged with upholding this freedom, it was Britain who controlled the Egyptian government. Moreover, the British government possessed the right to ignore the Convention while they continued in occupation, or in the event of a threat to Egypt's security. This virtually gave Britain a free hand. It was absurd, for instance, to imagine the Royal Navy allowing hostile warships to steam through the Canal to attack India or bombard Zanzibar. In addition, a threat to Egypt's security could well be interpreted to include local nationalist agitation.

It was also necessary to placate France. After all, it had been largely French capital and French initiative that had built the Canal. Now Britain had walked off with the prize. In real terms, however, France could pose no real threat to Britain's position. Diplomatic pin-pricks could be shrugged off, although the Fashoda Incident of 1898 was a more serious confrontation. In the meantime, French shareholders in the Canal Com-

pany received their dividends, and loans raised in Paris continued to be repaid. The Anglo-French entente of 1904, however, rationalised the situation. In return for Britain's acquiescence towards her ambitions in Morocco, France acknowledged her rival's Egyptian supremacy and stopped pestering for a time-limit to be set to the occupation.

While the British government was tidying up the diplomatic confusion caused by intervention, Anglo-Indian administrators in Cairo tackled the task of domestic reform. Liberal consciences were satisfied by an early assault on some of the cruder abuses of the Egyptian social system. The widespread use of flogging was banned, and after 1888 unpaid forced labour (especially that used to clean the canals) was partially abolished. French resistance to the abandonment of forced labour (the *corvée*) was only overcome after Cromer succeeded in balancing the Egyptian budget in 1888. A year later all interested European powers agreed to allow the Egyptian government to make laws applicable to all the inhabitants of Egypt, provided that these laws were not contrary to the various treaties and conventions already in existence. This gave Egypt a degree of legislative independence.

Perhaps the greatest British achievement in Egypt was the remarkable improvement in the irrigation system. Heavy loans were raised, and British engineers turned the Department of Public Works into an effective instrument of agricultural reform. Less success attended British efforts in the fields of education and justice. Indeed, there were complaints that such reforms as were introduced were aimed at improving the position of the British administration rather than leading to the advancement of Egyptians. Certainly the Civil Service was top-heavy with Englishmen, and Cromer's liberal convictions fell far short of encouraging Egyptian local autonomy. As a result there was a sharp increase in nationalist activity towards the end of Cromer's service in Egypt. This was hardly surprising, and it says much for Cromer's early success that the reaction was so long delayed.

The British presence in Egypt was both confused and splendidly effective. The confusion lay in Egypt's status, which in theory was that of an independent country

British influence evident at Port Said, 1892.

owing allegiance to the Turkish Sultan. It was not until the outbreak of the Great War, with Britain on one side and the Sultan on the other, that this somewhat ludicrous situation was rationalised by declaring Egypt a British protectorate. Before then it could have been described as a protected state, but this term had little constitutional significance.

Cromer's rank remained throughout Consul-General, his residence the comparatively modest consulate. Yet it was he whose approaching carriage could cause the Khedive to tremble; it was he who held the government in his hand. The Egyptian Cabinet, however, only contained one Englishman, and he was not allowed to vote. This concession to decorum could not disguise the fact that Cromer ran Egypt, without fuss, without histrionics, without waste. He was tactful, discreet, clear-headed and triumphantly reliable.

In other ways the British impact was less muted. The 6,000 men of the garrison forces marched through the streets of Cairo with bayonets fixed. A magnificent hotel, Shepheard's, provided British visitors with tea and cakes, and a refuge from the flies. There was even a British residential area in Cairo, and British social routine flourished undisturbed. Alexandria owed over three-quarters of its trade to British shipping. The Nile, the life-blood of the Egyptian peasant, provided tourists with the most leisurely way of viewing the past glories

of the Pharoahs – from the deck of a spotless steam boat.

Despite the apparently effortless imposition of British rule and British standards, despite the restoration of solvency, despite the undoubted improvements in administrative efficiency, the British experience in Egypt was in itself corrupting. Régimes were manipulated so shamelessly, Khedives overawed so easily, common Egyptians pushed out of the way so carelessly that, in the end, there was nothing for the British to respect in native Egypt. Archaeologists might stand in rapture before the well-preserved magnificence of the Pharaohs, but there seemed little in common between Rameses ii and a Khedive who combined an oriental taste for luxury with indebtedness to European bankers.

More than seventy years of occupation also left its mark. The tens of thousands of British troops who served in the Canal zone and Cairo must have brought back a ribald and contemptuous assessment of the Egyptians. Their experience of Egyptian society would hardly have included the progressive intellectuals of Alexandria, or Cairo's fastidious aristocrats. Instead, the impoverished and subdued peasantry (the fellahin), the cringing beggars, the purveyors of dubious pleasures, would have stuck in the mind. This impression, added to the continuing vital significance of the Suez Canal, made it difficult for the British to treat Egyptian nationalist aspirations seriously. It was therefore doubly humiliating when eventually a revolutionary Egyptian government (led by army colonels, like Arabi's movement three-quarters of a century before) abruptly ended Britain's control over the Canal and provoked an international crisis which revealed Britain's reduced powers in their proper light.

As a corollary to her position in Egypt, Britain had early become involved in the Sudan. Successive Egyptian governments had, from the beginning of the nineteenth century, conquered the Sudan piecemeal. By 1881 this enormous territory was ruled from Cairo through provincial governors. In that year, however, there began a revolutionary movement that was to have the most dramatic international repercussions. The revolution was headed by a man calling himself the Mahdi and enjoying veneration as a zealous religious reformer. The Mahdi, rallying around him the pious tribesmen of the Sudan, began to preach a holy war that would culminate in his elevation to the throne of the Turkish Sultans as the fountain-head of a purified Islam.

His sweeping early successes inevitably changed his crusade into a movement with strong political, even nationalist, overtones. The Egyptian governors of the Sudan, separated by huge distances, found themselves successively overwhelmed by the Mahdi and his followers. Between 1881 and 1882, the Egyptian government was plunged into deep crisis and unable to concentrate on events in the Sudan. The Mahdi, in the meantime, established his reputation for invincibility. When in 1883 the Egyptian government was able to move against the Mahdi, it did so disastrously. A raggle-taggle expeditionary force was dispatched under the joint command of Hicks Pasha (a retired Indian army officer) and a decrepit Egyptian general. Cromer grudged the expense of the expedition, and many of the most able Egyptian officers had been removed from command after the defeat of Arabi's movement. In November 1883, Hicks Pasha and his men were slaughtered by the dervishes.

The implications of this news shook both Cairo and London. The Egyptian army had been disbanded after the British conquest of 1882; if the Sudan was to be reconquered not only would this army have to be rebuilt, but substantial numbers of British troops would be needed. The Mahdi's success also made the withdrawal of the British garrisons in Egypt unlikely. The Gladstone government were in no mood to reconquer the Sudan for the benefit of Egypt. The Prime Minister, indeed, even spoke of the Sudanese as a people struggling rightly to be free. This enthusiasm for militant Islam perhaps owed something to the fear that a prolonged Sudan campaign might prove a bottomless pit into which desperately needed Egyptian revenue would be poured.

It was therefore imperative to evacuate the remaining Egyptian garrisons from the Sudan. To effect this withdrawal Gladstone chose Major-General Charles Gordon. Gordon was an eccentric character who had built up a high public reputation through a free-booting and extraordinary military career. Seeing himself as the sword-bearer of evangelical Christianity, Gordon had served unusual causes. His brilliantly unorthodox leadership of the Emperor of China's forces against local rebels had earned him the nickname 'Chinese Gordon'. He had subsequently served as Governor-General of the Sudan under the Khedive Ismail. He had thus seemed, not least to certain British newspaper editors, an ideal candidate to supervise the withdrawal from the Sudan.

This enthusiasm, however, took no account of Gordon's perversity. He was every bit as convinced of his own righteousness as was the Mahdi. Solitary, visionary, and obstinate, Gordon had an equally strong taste for brandy and for independent action. Once at Khartoum, and under an arguably vague mandate, he decided to stay put. There is evidence that he even

Death of an imperial hero! A deserted General Gordon surrounded by dervish vultures. The fall of Khartoum in 1885 caused a great public protest in Britain.

contemplated leading the reconquest from the embattled Sudanese capital.

By May 1884 it was quite clear that a major military expedition would be needed to raise the siege of Khartoum. Gordon himself called for reinforcements. The Gladstone government was torn in two by the predicament. Eventually a relief expedition under Garnett Wolseley began a slow progress down the Nile. Two days before the paddle-steamers sighted Khartoum, however, the city had been stormed and its garrison massacred by the dervishes. Gordon lay mutilated among those whom he had refused to abandon.

On 5 February 1885 the news reached England. A shocked and sometimes hysterical reaction ensued. In death, Gordon assumed even more heroic proportions. This was no Hicks Pasha blundering to self-destruction, but a lily-white national hero cut down in his prime by murderous fanatics. The Queen was incensed, and the copious underlinings in her almost frantic letters grew even more determined. The Cabinet contemplated resignation. Gladstone was singled out for venomous abuse. For several weeks crowds gathered outside 10 Downing Street to hoot and jeer, and stones were flung through the windows. In the music halls the 'Grand Old Man' was presented as the 'Murderer of Gordon'. The furore undoubtedly brought Gladstone's government near to its fall, although this did not come about till the Irish Nationalists withdrew their support, for entirely different reasons, in June 1885.

The next year was occupied with the profound political convulsions centring on the Irish Home Rule crisis. When eventually Lord Salisbury emerged at the head of a stable administration in June 1886 there was little to be done but to abandon the Sudan to Mahdism. For a decade, successive British governments steered clear of intervention. One reason for this inactivity was the optimistic assumption that Mahdism would decay sufficiently to allow a bloodless re-occupation. But even after the death of the Mahdi in 1885, shortly after Gordon's murder, the Sudan remained hostile and resilient. Recognising that a reconquest would probably be costly and prolonged, the Rosebery government proclaimed a protectorate over Uganda in 1894 with at least half

Kitchener as Sidar of the
Egyptian army. It was
Kitchener who avenged
Gordon's death in the
Sudan campaign of
1896–9

an eye on its possible use as an invasion base.

As it happened, the Sudan was reconquered from the north. In 1896 Italian forces engaged in an attempt to annex Abyssinia were humiliatingly crushed at a great battle at Adowa. The Abyssinian army had been helped towards its triumph by French and Russian military advice and assistance. Moreover, the victorious King Menelek seemed likely to forge an alliance with the dervishes of the Sudan. The British government was thus faced with the double threat of unwelcome European influence in East Africa and an inconvenient alliance between two independent African countries. Britain was forced to take immediate action, and a little over a week after the battle of Adowa, Salisbury announced the invasion of the Sudan.

The first official justifications for the Anglo-Egyptian move dwelt heavily on the urgent need to relieve the besieged Italian garrison at Kassala. Despite this sudden manifestation of concern for fellow-Europeans and fellow-imperialists, the main reason for intervention was the very real fear that other nations might become involved in the Sudan. Control of the Sudan would mean that pressure could be put on Egypt through a threat to manipulate the life-giving waters of the Upper Nile. Rather than take this risk Britain and Egypt moved against the dervishes.

The Anglo-Egyptian forces were commanded by Kitchener, who had played a conspicuous part in the fateful Gordon relief expedition. Rigid, unrelenting, single-minded, and obsessed with detail, Kitchener retained an icy reserve even under the blazing desert sun. However, he wished passionately to avenge Gordon, and had now been given the support from London and Cairo to do it. Efficiently, gradually, and unremarkably, Kitchener fought his way down the Nile, and eventually confronted the dervish host at Omdurman close by Khartoum.

The battle of Omdurman took place on 2 September 1898. Although very much to the taste of the British public, and enlivened by the futile (though well-chronicled) charge of the 21st Lancers, the battle was little short of a predictable rout. The massed forces of the Khalifa (the Mahdi's successor) were badly led and armed with primitive weapons. Thousands of dervishes obligingly ran full tilt at the well-served rifles and maxim guns. The Anglo-Egyptian army lost forty-eight men, but over 11,000 of the enemy were left dead upon the battlefield.

Khartoum was occupied, and Gordon's self-imposed martyrdom revenged. Kitchener's deportment in his hour of triumph was both callous and tender. He wept for Gordon's memory, but ordered the desecration of the Mahdi's tomb and toyed with the idea of using the dead leader's skull as an inkstand or goblet. Sections of British opinion were horrified, and Kitchener made haste to reassure the Queen and disarm his critics. An ugly impression persisted, however, and was strengthened by rumours that the victorious army had looted, and had murdered wounded dervishes. Kitchener's disclaimers were counterbalanced by evidence that after the battle he had repeatedly called 'Cease fire! Cease fire! Cease fire! Oh, what a dreadful waste of ammunition!'

The Sudan campaign was soon to provide more matter for debate. A little up the Nile at Fashoda, a French engineer, Captain Marchand, and a few companions, had hoisted the tricolour! Their object had originally been to find the site for a possible dam to divert the waters of the Nile. This rather extravagant project was soon shown to be impractical as well. But the confrontation between the advancing Anglo-Egyptian forces and Marchand sparked off a diplomatic incident of enormous proportions. Fed by intense public indignation in both countries, the crisis brought Britain and France stumbling to the edge of war. In the Sudan, Kitchener had dealt with the matter pragmatically by inviting Marchand aboard his paddle-steamer and treating him with unusual forbearance.

The British and French governments eventually settled their differences in the Sudan by agreeing on a border between Sudanese and French territory. The frontier admittedly preserved British interests to the full, but then Britain held all the trump cards during the crisis. For his part, Kitchener spent the year after Omdurman in mopping up dervish resistance and wielding rather autocratic and abrupt powers as Governor-General of the Sudan. The Khalifa and his surviving emirs were hunted down and shot. The civil

Colonel Marchand. His confrontation with Kitchener after Omdurman was the occasion for the Fashoda Crisis of 1898.

The Sudanese reconquest complete. The bodies of the Khalifa (the Mahdi's successor) and other dervish leaders after they had been hunted down in November 1899.

administration of the Sudan was reorganised, and British officials recruited.

The constitutional status of the Sudan was confirmed in 1899 as a condominium. In theory it had been Egyptian territory that Kitchener had reconquered. Both Britain and Egypt were now declared jointly responsible for its government. However, since Britain effectively ruled Egypt, the partnership was clearly less than equal. In its half century of condominium status, the Sudan never had an Egyptian Governor-General, and the Civil Service was dominated by Englishmen. In these circumstances the condominium was only a constitutional fig-leaf, designed to limit the embarrassment of all the parties involved. Unfortunately the fig-leaf was as transparent as many of the other devices employed to disguise the exercise of Imperial power.

11 The Scramble for Empire

The Far East: expansion in Malaya and the Pacific; the penetration of China; the crushing of the Boxer Rebellion. Economic depression in the West Indies, and the Norman Commission of 1897. The partition of Africa: a discussion of the motives behind the partition; 'Indirect Rule', and the 'white man's burden'; the economic and administrative problems of the new colonies.

BY THE END of the Victorian Age those territories in Asia, Africa, or the Pacific that had escaped European annexation or domination could be counted on the fingers of one hand. In Africa, Abyssinia the fastness of the lion of Judah remained independent; so did the freed-slave foundation of Liberia. In Asia, Siam balanced uneasily between British and French interests; Afghanistan also clung to its autonomy despite periodic bullying by the government of India; neither China nor Persia could be considered as truly independent nations. At the edge of the Asian land-mass there was, however, one country of such strength and vitality that the great European powers either eyed it warily or courted it diplomatically; but Japan was an almost ludicrously successful exception to a world-wide pattern.

Elsewhere in the Far East, the British Empire had taken its share of the pickings. Most of Malaya was under the influence of British Residents or directly ruled by the Colonial Office. In 1896 the Federation of Malay States had brought the 'advised' territories into a loose union. But the Crown Colonies of Singapore and Penang had stayed out of this organisation. In theory the Sultans of the Federated States retained their sovereignty; in practice a British Resident-General at Kuala Lumpur had executive control.

To the east of the Malay peninsula, Britain controlled (in different ways) three more territories. These were Brunei, North Borneo and Sarawak. In Brunei the

Plain speaking. John Bull to disrespectful Frenchman: 'Look here, my little Friend. I don't want to hurt your little feelings – but, COME OFF THAT FLAG!!!' In fact, African partition, although often a cause of conflict, was usually accomplished by reasonable treaties.

Sultan was protected by the British government; in Sarawak the Sultan *was* British, and known as Rajah Brooke; North Borneo was ruled by a Chartered Company. These territories provided rubber and oil. The Malay states produced rubber too, as well as tin. Both were valuable commodities for re-export. Singapore was for south east Asia what Hong Kong was for the China Sea – a gigantic entrepôt for British commerce.

Although Britain had initially become involved in the Malay mainland in order to safeguard the trade route to China, her involvement in the Pacific lacked any such consistent self-interest. Indeed, it is difficult to discern any coherent or enthusiastic policy behind the acquisition of south-eastern New Guinea, Fiji, Tonga, the Cook Islands, or other smaller island groups. Broadly speaking, Britain had extended her influence over these territories either for humanitarian reasons or because of Australian and New Zealand pressure. Appropriately, Britain had willingly allowed Australians to administer Papua and New Zealanders the Cook Islands. After the Great War she was to abandon even more responsibility to her Pacific Dominions.

In China, Britain had continued to pursue a policy of uncomplicated aggression in the defence of her commercial interests. Kowloon, opposite Hong Kong, had been ceded in 1861. Growing European intervention had encouraged Britain to take the mainland New Territories on a ninety-nine year lease in 1898, and in the same year to acquire the potential naval base at Wei-hai-Wei. These moves were made chiefly to coun-

Empire in the Pacific. Parade of Fiji Constabulary beneath the Union Jack.

Crushing of Boxer Rebellion, 1900. A French cartoon satirises the European powers in unholy alliance.

The reward for rebellion. A captured Boxer about to be decapitated before an audience of European troops.

terbalance the establishment of the Russian naval base at Port Arthur and a German base at Kiau-chau. Apart from territorial possession, Britain's hand lay heavily on China at the end of the century. The head of the Imperial Chinese Customs was an Irishman, Robert Hart. The international port of Shanghai showed clear signs of British influence. The once despised foreigners had now assumed the deportment of the heaven-born.

Such unashamed domination by the European powers, the United States, and Japan, was likely to provoke a sharp reaction. The reaction came with the Boxer rising of 1898–1900. In 1898 China was still reeling from its humiliatingly swift defeat by Japan in the 1894–5 war. Discontent was centred in the province of Shantung where economic depression had been exacerbated by two years of famine as well as disastrous flooding by the Yellow river. Among the Shantung peasantry these natural catastrophes could easily be attributed to foreign disregard for the Chinese spirits of earth and water. Christian missionaries were as unpopular as the European governments that supported them.

Early in 1898 the Boxers came out into the open. Drawing on the tough Shantung peasantry, the movement indulged in optimistic assessments of its own strength and cultivated the weird mumbo-jumbo of a secret society. By late 1899 the Boxers had won the powerful support of the Dowager Empress Tz'u-hsi who hoped to unleash them upon the foreigners. Subsequently a number of missionaries and converts were killed, and the heads of the Japanese and German legations in Pekin murdered. On 21 June 1900 the Chinese government declared war on the foreign powers and the Boxers besieged the legation in Pekin.

The reaction in Europe to these events was out of all proportion to the facts. Under a thousand foreign diplomats and soldiers, and about 3,000 Chinese Christians were in the three-acre compound of the legations. The Dowager Empress failed to carry the majority of her provincial governors with her, and her Commander-in-Chief deliberately withheld modern guns from the besiegers, thus making the fall of the legations unlikely.

The London *Daily Mail*, however, published in July a horrifying and completely erroneous account of the destruction of the legations and the accompanying massacre. This fabricated dispatch perhaps helped to prod the foreign powers into determined action. By August 1900 an army of over 20,000 foreign troops had relieved the Pekin legations. By late 1900 there were more than 45,000 foreign troops in North China. The Dowager Empress fled to remote Sian, and the Boxers and their supporters were subjected to ruthless treatment by the victorious powers.

The victors chose, however, to preserve the Chinese dynasty. They also preserved their privileged position

Destitution in the
West Indies occasioned
the Norman Commission
of 1897. The dried-up
river at Port of Spain,
Trinidad.

within the system. In a display of unity as impressive as it was untypical, the British, French, German, Russian, Japanese, Italian and United States' governments had once more defeated Chinese opposition. The ease with which this had been done was both an encouragement to the foreign powers and a further source of humiliation for the vanquished. Chinese nationalist movements in the twentieth century were to find potent inspiration in the somewhat incoherent and quickly cowed Boxer Rebellion.

In the last few years of the nineteenth century the British government displayed unprecedented concern for the plight of the West Indies. Since the early 1800's the once prosperous sugar islands had been afflicted with economic depression and social and political confusion. Although quick to intervene in the Jamaica Rebellion of 1865, Whitehall was less inclined to offer economic assistance to impoverished communities. Indeed it was generally accepted in the Colonial Office that Crown Colonies must make their own way in economic matters. If a colony prospered it would receive the rewards of success in improved facilities and perhaps in a measure of local autonomy. If, however, a colony floundered in debt and unemployment it could expect little material assistance from Britain.

The advent of Joseph Chamberlain to the Colonial Office in 1895 radically altered this philosophy. Chamberlain saw the tropical Crown Colonies as undeveloped estates of the realm; ripe for investment and for economic growth. Although his assessment of their potential was perhaps over-optimistic, his policy was at least positive and constructive. The West Indies provided him with an ideal field in which to exercise his initiative.

Chamberlain lost no time in appointing a Royal Commission to the West Indies. Led by Sir Henry Norman, the Commission investigated the British Caribbean in 1897. Its report was insistent that industries (such as fruit growing) should be encouraged as alternatives to the prevailing hazardous reliance upon sugar. It was also recommended that nearly £600,000 should be loaned and granted to the West Indies. Despite the misgivings of some of his Cabinet colleagues on this score, Chamberlain announced in 1898 a five-year plan for West Indian reconstruction.

Not only was the financial assistance recommended by the Norman Commission used to alleviate local distress and improve island communications, but some was set aside to encourage new industries. In addition, Chamberlain established the Department of Tropical Agriculture, as well as Schools of Tropical Medicine in London and Liverpool. In this way the government gave its backing to necessary research work, and to improving farming methods in the West Indian islands. In 1902 Chamberlain succeeded in his objective of dismantling the system whereby certain European nations subsidised, through bounties, the production of local beet sugar. The Brussels agreement of that year ended the bounty system and gave some relief to the British West Indies where sugar went unsubsidised.

These measures did not transform the West Indian economies overnight. The blight of neglect and mismanagement could not be so easily exorcised, and unemployment and low incomes proved endemic. But a start had been made, and some improvement was soon evident. To have put similar programmes into operation throughout the Empire, however, would have required a freer purse than Westminster's, and a succession of Colonial Secretaries as dynamic as Chamberlain. Failing these requirements, the dependent Empire could expect little immediate assistance.

Yet the last two decades of the nineteenth century saw a huge acquisition of British territory – chiefly in Africa. Why was the British government, usually so fastidious

Germany as a competitor for colonies. Captain Hermann of the 1898 Tanganyika Boundary Commission.

Refugees from French
West Africa. King and
elders of Katenu seek
British protection.

in its annexations, impelled to scramble for hitherto
uncoveted tracts of land? In some ways, of course,
British policymakers displayed a leisurely approach
which contrasted sharply with the hungry appetites of
parvenu colonial powers like Germany or Italy. Lord
Salisbury was prepared to pass Tanganyika over to
Bismarck with a well-bred and indifferent wave of the
hand. One cannot imagine Balfour losing much sleep
over Carl Peter's freebooting expeditions for Imperial
Germany.

Nonetheless, the tally of British acquisitions in Africa
between 1880 and 1902 was impressive: Egypt, the
Sudan, Somaliland, Uganda, Kenya, Zanzibar, Northern and Southern Rhodesia, Nyasaland, Bechuanaland,
much of Nigeria, the Gold Coast's hinterland, and
finally the Orange Free State and the Transvaal. The
driving forces behind this massive extension of empire
are diverse and a matter for some historical dispute.

It has been traditionally acceptable to interpret the
African scramble in terms of heightened European

rivalries – Britain jumping in ahead of Germany, France forestalling Italy, and the like. While this theory is neat, and undoubtedly convincing in some cases, it tends to ignore clashes between European and African nationalisms. For instance, was not Britain drawn into her two most spectacular commitments chiefly by the need to control both Egyptian and Afrikaner nationalism? In addition, there is growing evidence that black nationalism, or at least tribalism, was frequently a local factor requiring intervention. Finally, what could (say) Germany, Italy, Belgium, even France, have achieved against resolute action by the Royal Navy? How would they effectively have annexed their cherished colonies?

Another theory is that pressing economic incentives, in the form of new markets and sources of raw materials, occasioned the African partition. Here again, the evidence is not wholly convincing, despite the dual assurances of the radical English theorist J. A. Hobson and Vladimir Ilyitch Lenin. While it is true that between 1865 and 1894 British trade with tropical Africa doubled, it also doubled with South America and Australia, and with South Africa it trebled. Moreover, the *proportion* of British trade with tropical Africa actually declined during the 1890's. Between 1865-90 this proportion of the whole of Britain's trade was a mere 0·80%; but between 1890-4 it shrank to 0·77%.

It is nevertheless true that powerful economic lobbies and persuasive capitalist propagandists urged the British

Indian coolie labour building the Uganda railway. Large numbers of Indians entered British East African possessions as indentured labourers.

Mwanga, Kabaka of Buganda. His kingdom retained a privileged status within the Protectorate of Uganda.

The Ashanti War 1873–4. British troops riding in on the Gold Coast surf.

government to seize new territories in Africa. How much notice Lord Salisbury took of these advocacies is open to question. The left wing of the Liberal party certainly suspected the Rand millionaires of forcing the Boer War on the nation. For a middle-of-the-road Liberal opinion of the African scramble one is left with Campbell-Bannerman's judgement, in 1899, that 'The danger of a good deal of this expansiveness . . . is that it withdraws the energies and enterprises of our countrymen from markets which they used to control . . . in the vain pursuit of what is little more than a will-o'-the-wisp . . . of a market which does not exist'.

More convincing than the economic argument, perhaps, is the thesis that Britain's role in the African partition was shaped by the need to preserve the Suez route to the old Empire in India and Australasia. While this is naturally not relevant in the case of West Africa, an examination of the motives behind the acquisition of Britain's East African Empire reinforces the thesis. There is no doubt that many British statesmen became virtually obsessed with the need to secure the Suez Canal and to protect the Indian Empire. Consequently territories bordering on Egypt were jealously guarded, and, if necessary, annexed. In this sense, imperial expansion in much of Africa was essentially defensive.

Once possessed of a vast African Empire in the tropics, the British seemed uncertain what to do with it. Certain cash crops immediately lent themselves to development, others could be introduced. But how far could the new colonies ever become settled by Europeans? The Kenya Highlands attracted a few thousand white pioneers, whose success later encouraged speculation that a new settler-dominion could be carved out of East Africa. But the Gold Coast and Nigeria seemed unlikely environments for immigrants from Glasgow and Manchester. Indeed the British government, far from hurling every available scrap of human and financial investment into the tropical African Empire, seemed content to leave it near the bottom of the imperial pyramid. In 1903 the Colonial Office even offered Uganda to the Zionist movement as a Jewish homeland!

Admittedly there were, by the beginning of the twentieth century, some signs that the new territories would be given a degree of administrative order. Crown Colony government was a predictable and recognisable form. In addition, 'Indirect Rule' was eventually

WHITE SLAVES OR BLACK?

Mr. Zanzibar:—"FROM WHAT I CAN SEE, MRS. BRITANNIA, IT WOULD BE JUST AS WELL FOR YOU TO REMEDY SOME MATTERS AT HOME, BEFORE INTERFERING SO ACTIVELY ABROAD."

Imperialism abroad or Reform at home? The dilemma expressed in a cartoon of 1875.

to give a still greater degree of uniformity. Given its African expression in Lord Lugard's work in northern Nigeria, the formula of 'Indirect Rule' was a compound of firm supervision from the Colonial government with the delegation of much local administration to African chieftains. Although not particularly progressive, this system was inexpensive to operate and at least left some indigenous institutions intact. That it tended to preserve African obscurantism and shore up traditionalism was not at first noticed, or if noticed, deemed perfectly respectable.

Lugard's work took some time to make its mark. Although by the 1920's the African colonies were attracting an appropriate share of the abler administrators, this had not been the case at the turn of the century when the Indian and Sudan Civil Services had taken off the cream. While much had been made at the end of Victoria's reign of the white man's burden, few had seemed willing to shoulder it in Africa. Even when this situation altered, the long-term prospects of the tropical African Empire were at best unclear and at worst unpromising.

How far did Britain exploit her dependent colonies? It is easy to assume that a gross manipulation of colonial economies was the hallmark of all European imperial powers. Looked at dispassionately the facts by no means confirm this analysis. Of course, the Indian cotton industry declined sharply in the nineteenth century in the face of privileged competition from Lancashire; a few private companies were able to give a huge dividend

Far-flung power. A British engineer instructs labourers at the naval base of Wei-hai-Wei, acquired in 1898 from China.

on investment. Not a great deal of the profits of trade were ploughed back into colonial economies; most tribal societies saw no dramatic rise in the standard of living.

Yet it would be a mistake to imagine British capitalists wantonly plundering dependent lands. They certainly sought profits, but these were often no greater than profits from industries established in non-colonial territories. Dividends from capital investment could be higher from Argentine railways than from Ugandan rubber. The Chinese economy was hardly treated with greater respect than that of the Gold Coast. Moreover, Britain's adherence to free trade theoretically gave her no greater commercial advantage in her own colonies than any other nation. Indeed, looking back at the Victorian dependent Empire one is struck by the low level of investment, the absence of systematic economic development.

Perhaps more damaging than economic domination was the commonplace assumption that all Africans were savages and unfitted for self-government. Not only was this assumption somewhat at odds with the principles of 'Indirect Rule', but it ignored the fact that before the advent of Europeans, Africans had indeed governed themselves. Frequently the government had been rough, even barbarous, but it had worked. Perhaps missionaries and colonial administrators exaggerated the defects of African self-rule in order to justify their own activities. Certainly the very real achievements of African civilisation from Ghana to Zimbabwe were scandalously ignored.

By the beginning of the twentieth century, therefore, the British Empire had acquired huge fresh territorial responsibilities, mainly in Africa and the Pacific, but had not yet fully adjusted to the fact. Ironically by the time that a measure of administrative uniformity had been stamped upon these colonies, the reasons for their original annexation had often become less relevant. British national interests had changed, and the pretexts for African dominion suffered accordingly. The late-Victorians had acquired a colonial empire that their descendants were to neglect for half a century and then abandon within a single decade.

Epilogue

THE BOUNDARIES of the British Empire were not at their widest at the end of Queen Victoria's reign. After the Great War a number of mandated territories were brought into the Empire. In Africa, Tanganyika and parts of Togoland and the Cameroons came under British rule; south-west Africa was handed over to the Union of South Africa. What amounted to a new Empire was carved out of the Middle East, where Palestine, Transjordan and Mesopotamia (later called Iraq) became British responsibilities. In the Pacific, German New Guinea was taken, and Australia and New Zealand acquired long-coveted German islands.

Although Britain theoretically administered her new acquisitions under the mandate of the League of Nations, in practice she treated them much as if they were ordinary parts of her Colonial Empire. The strips of Togoland and the Cameroons were simply tacked on to existing British colonies in west Africa; Tanganyika effectively became a Crown Colony, Mesopotamia a Protected State. In all, the mandated territories totalled nearly one million square miles in area, and contained about 13,000,000 inhabitants. Almost an afterthought of Empire, the mandates nonetheless carried considerable human and material implications. Mesopotamia was rich in oil, Palestine rich in potential conflict. The Middle Eastern mandates in particular were to prove troublesome responsibilities, and a drain on Britain's imperial energies.

In the 1920's the newly extended Empire already exhibited clear indications of its eventual decline and fall. Nationalism was rampant in India and Egypt, and a powerful factor in Ceylon and Mesopotamia. The first flickerings of African nationalism could be observed in Kenya and the Gold Coast. The Irish Free State was a Dominion of truculent disposition, and only grudgingly remained within the Empire. The other Dominions, having been treated as independent states during the 1919 Peace negotiations, were inclined to act as independent states in the post-war world.

Britain had expended colossal quantities of resolve and wealth in order to win the Great War. This had left her weaker not only as a world power, but also as an Imperial power. Perhaps the will to rule subject people suffered as a result. The rapid growth of the Labour movement after 1918 also meant that one of Britain's two great political parties was in theory strongly anti-imperialist. Elsewhere the Soviet Union (by conviction) and the United States (from habit) could be counted as formidable opponents of European imperialism. Although patriots were still able to sing *Rule Britannia* with gusto, the plain truth was that the golden age of the British Empire had passed shortly after the death of Queen Victoria.

Bibliography

A full bibliography would comprise many hundreds of volumes. The following are some of the books, mostly of recent publication, that the author has found particularly useful. All books are published in London unless otherwise stated.

GENERAL

Beloff, M.	*Imperial Sunset* (1969)
Bennett, C. (ed.)	*The Concept of Empire* (2nd ed. 1962)
Cambridge History of the British Empire, Vol. 3 (1959)	
	(Cambridge)
Carrier, N. H. and	
Jeffery, J. R.	*External Migration* (1953)
Fieldhouse, D. K.	*The Colonial Empires* (1966)
	The Theory of Capitalist Imperialism (1967)
Fraser, P.	*Joseph Chamberlain* (1966)
Gordon, D. C.	*The Dominion Partnership in Imperial Defense* (1965)
	(Baltimore)
Judd, D.	*Balfour and the British Empire* (1968)
Kendle, J. E.	*The Colonial and Imperial Conferences 1887–1911* (1967)
Kiernan, V. G.	*The Lords of Human Kind* (1969)
Lowe, C. J.	*The Reluctant Imperialists*, Vols. 1 and 2 (1967)
Mansergh, N.	*The Commonwealth Experience* (1969)
Morrell, W. P.	*British Colonial Policy in the Mid-Victorian Age* (1969)
	(Oxford)
Morris, J.	*Pax Britannica* (1968)
Porter, B.	*Critics of Empire* (1968)
Thornton, A. P.	*The Imperial Idea and Its Enemies* (1959)

CANADA

Creighton, D.	*Dominion of the North* (New ed. 1958)
	The Road to Confederation (1964) (Toronto)
Graham, G. S.	*Empire of the North Atlantic* (1958) (Toronto)
Macdonald, N.	*Canada: Immigration & Colonization 1841–1903* (1966)
	(Aberdeen)
New, C.	*Lord Durham's Mission to Canada* (1929, Oxford) (Rpt Ottawa 1963)

Preston, R. A.	*Canada and 'Imperial Defense'* (1967) (Durham, N.C.)
Schull, J.	*Laurier: The First Canadian* (1965) (Toronto)
Wade, F. M.	*The French Canadians 1760–1945* (1956) (Toronto)

AUSTRALIA AND NEW ZEALAND

Burroughs, P.	*Britain and Australia 1831–55* (1967) (Oxford)
Condliffe, J. B.	*New Zealand in the Making* (Rev. ed. 1959)
La Nauze, J. A.	*Alfred Deakin*, 2 Vols (1965) (Melbourne)
Miller, H.	*New Zealand* (1950)
Pike, D.	*Paradise of Dissent, South Australia 1829–57* (1957)
Shaw, A. G. L.	*Convicts and Colonies* (1966)
	The Story of Australia (1955)
Sinclair, K.	*A History of New Zealand* (1961)
	The Origins of the Maori Wars (1957) (Wellington)
Ward, J. M.	*Empire in the Antipodes* (1966)

SOUTH AFRICA

Fisher, J.	*The Afrikaners* (1969)
Galbraith, J. S.	*Reluctant Empire: British Policy on the South African Frontier 1843–54* (1963) (California)
Hancock, W. K.	*Smuts*, Vol. 1 (1962) (Cambridge)
Kiewiet de, C. W.	*The Imperial Factor in South Africa* (1937) (Cambridge)
Kruger, R.	*Goodbye Dolly Gray* (1959)
Le May, G. H. L.	*British Supremacy in South Africa 1899–1907* (1965) (Oxford)
Lockhart, J. G. and Woodhouse, G. M.	*Rhodes* (1963)
Marais, J. S.	*The Fall of Kruger's Republic* (1961) (Oxford)
Pakenham, E.	*Jameson's Raid* (1960)
Roberts, B.	*Cecil Rhodes and the Princess* (1969)
The Oxford History of South Africa, Vol. 1, ed. Wilson and Thompson (1969) (Oxford)
Van Jaarsveld, F. A.	*The Making of Afrikaner Nationalism* (1961) (Cape Town)
Walker, E. A.	*The Great Trek* (1934)
	A History of Southern Africa (3rd ed. 1957)

INDIA

Dilks, D.	*Curzon*: Vol. 1 The Years of Achievement (1969), Vol. 2 Frustration (1970)
Edwardes, M.	*British India* (1967)
	High Noon of Empire (1965)

Gopal, S.	*British Policy in India 1858–1905* (1965)
Greenberger, A.J.	*The British Image of India* (1969)
Mehrotra, S.R.	*India and the Commonwealth* (1965)
Moore, R.J.	*Sir Charles Wood's India Policy 1853–66* (1966) (Manchester)
	Liberalism and Indian Politics 1872–1922 (1966)
Stokes, E.	*The English Utilitarians and India* (1959) (Oxford)

THE COLONIAL EMPIRE

Burns, A.	*A History of the British West Indies* (1954)
Fage, J.D.	*An Introduction to the History of West Africa* (3rd ed. 1962) (Cambridge)
Fairbank, J.K.	*Trade and Diplomacy on the China Coast* (1953) (Cambridge, Mass.)
Flint, J.E.	*Sir George Goldie and the Making of Nigeria* (1960) (Oxford)
Hargreaves, J.D.	*Prelude to the Partition of West Africa* (1963)
History of East Africa Vol. 1 (1963), Vol. 2 (1965) (Oxford)	
Ingham, K.	*A History of East Africa* (1962)
Morrell, W.P.	*Britain in the Pacific Islands* (1960) (Oxford)
Oliver, R.	*Sir Harry Johnston and the Scramble for Africa* (1957)
Robinson, R. and	
Gallagher, J.	*Africa and the Victorians* (1961)
Semmel, B.	*Jamaican Blood and Victorian Conscience* (1963) (Cambridge)
Williams, E.	*British Historians and the West Indies* (1966)
Woodcock, G.	*The British in the Far East* (1969)

EGYPT AND THE SUDAN

Al-Sayyid, A.L.	*Egypt and Cromer;* A Study in Anglo-Egyptian Relations (1968)
Holt, P.M.	*Egypt and the Fertile Crescent* (1966)
	A Modern History of the Sudan (1961)
Kinross, Lord	*Between Two Seas* (1968)
Magnus, P.	*Kitchener; Portrait of an Imperialist* (1958)
Pudney, J.	*Suez: De Lesseps' Canal* (1968)
Sanderson, G.N.	*England, Europe and the Upper Nile 1882–99* (1965) (Edinburgh)
Tignor, R.L.	*Modernization and British Colonial Rule in Egypt 1882–1914* (1966) (Princeton)

Index

Figures in bold type indicate illustrations

Abdur Rahman, Amir, 168
Aborigines Committee (1837), 9
Aden, 95, 116
Adowa, battle of (1896), 199
Afghanistan, **71**, 81, **181**: British invasions (1839 and 1879), 70–2, 166–8
Afrikaners, the, 55–8, 65–7, 66, 148, 150, 155; Orange Free State and Transvaal republics, 60, 62–4, 147–8; in Cape Colony, 63, 151; and South African War (1899–1902), 157; after the war, 162, 163 *See also* Great Trek
Alberta, 130
Alexandria, bombardment of (1882), 188–9, **189**
Anti-Corn Law League, 10
Antigua, 98
Arabi, Colonel, **187**: leads revolt in Egypt, 187–90, 194
Ascension, 95
Ashanti War (1873–4), **211**
Asquith, H. H., 11
Atkinson, (Sir) Harry, 145
Auckland, Lord, 70–2
Australia, 30–43, 136–42: immigrants, 9, 35, **36**, 36–8, **138**, 139: transportation of convicts, 31–4, **32–3**, **35**, 42; gold rush, 35–8, **37**; urban overcrowding, 38–9; aborigines, **38**, 39; squatters, 39, 41; bush-rangers, 40–2; internal self-government for colonies, 42–3, **43**; contributions to naval defence, 120–1; trading boom, **136**, .136–8; federation movement, 139–40; Commonwealth comes into being, 140–2, **142**

Bahamas, the, 104

Balfour, Arthur (Earl of Balfour), 127, 155, 177, **181**, 209: and Cabinet Defence Committee, 122; and Tariff Reform, 124; and the Uitlanders, 155–6; and Curzon, 180–2
Baluchi chieftains, **178**
Bamangwato, the, 58
Bantu, the, 55, 57, 61, 63
Barbados, 98, 99, 104: stamps, **8**
Baring, Sir Evelyn (Earl of Cromer), Consul-General in Egypt, 190–3, **191**, 195
Barton, Sir Edmund, 127
Basutoland, 65
Bechuanaland, 151, 153, 209
Bengal Army, sepoys, 78
Bentham, Jeremy and Benthamite radicals, 11, 98
Bermuda, 104
Bismarck, 209
Bloemfontein, 67: Convention (1854), 60
Blood River, battle of, 59
Boer War, *see* South African War
Boers, the, *see* Afrikaners
Botha, General Louis, 158, **158**, 163
Boxer rising, **205**, 205–7
British Columbia, 11, 24, 27, 130; waggon trail, **26**
British East India Company, 68, 70, 72–3, 75–6, 78–81, **79**, 84, 89, 107, 110
British Guiana, 104
British North America Act (1867), 28–9
British South Africa Company, 14, 151
British West Indies, 95, 98–105, 207–8: slavery and emancipation, **94**, 98–101, 99; sugar trade, 98–100, 207–8; Jamaica Rebellion, *see* separate entry; Crown Colony rule in many islands, 104

Brooke, Sir James, Rajah of Sarawak, 107, 204
Browne, Thomas Gore, 52
Brunei, 203–4
Buller, Charles, 18, 98
Buller, Sir Redvers, 157
Burgers, President of Transvaal, 148
Burma: conquest of Lower Burma, 75; conquest of Upper Burma, 168, **169**: province of India, 168–9
Burns, John, 161
Bushmen, the, 59

Cabinet Defence Committee, 122
Cameroons, the, 215
Campbell-Bannerman, Sir Henry, 160, 162, 211
Canada, 16–29, 64, 121, 130–6: Upper and Lower Canada, 16, 17, 23, 27, 29; English and French-speaking subjects, 16–21, 133; 'rebellions' (1837), 17–18, **18**, 24; Durham Report 9, 18, 20, 24; Canadian society, 21–2, **22**, **26**; immigrants, 9, 22–3, 131–3; Act of Union (1840), 24; prairie fires, **25**; commercial treaty with U.S.A., 25; tariff on steel, 26; federation, 28–9, **29**; imperial preferences and tariff reform, 124, 134; Canadian Pacific Railway, **128**, 130–1; new provinces. 130
Canning, Lord ('Clemency' Canning), 80, 92
Canning, Sir Stratford, 111
Cape Colony, 9, 11, 17, 55–8, 61–3, 65, 121, 151, 158: stamps, **8**; abolition of slavery, 57–8; representative government, 60–4
Cape Town, 67, **67**
Carlyle, Thomas, 101, 104

Carnarvon, Lord, 64, 147, 148
Cartier, (Sir) George, 28
Cetewayo, Zulu chief, 147, **148**
Ceylon, 95, 105–6, **106**, 116, 117, 216: racial problems, 105; constitutional progress, 105–6
Chaka, Zulu chief, **62**
Chamberlain, Joseph, 7, 11, 14, **114**, 119–20, 126–7, **127**, 140, 155–6, 158, 163, **163**, 188, 207–8: and tariff reform, **123**, 123–5, 134; and Jameson Raid, 153, 155
Chartered territories, 116
China, British interests in, 107–8, 204–7: opium trade, 107; treaty ports, 107–8; Boxer rising, **205**, 205–7
Christiansburg slave-trading fortress, **104**
Clive, Robert, 68
Cobden, Richard and Cobdenite Radicals, 11, 20, 97
Colonial Conferences, 14, 126–7, **127**, 134
Colonial Defence Committee, 121–2
Committee of Imperial Defence, 122, 161
Consolidated Goldfields Ltd., 151
Cook, Capt. James, 31
Cook Islands, 204
Corn Laws, abolition of, 10, 25
Corn Tax (1902), 124
Cromer, Earl of, see Baring
Crown, position of the, 116–17
Crown Colonies, 116
Curzon of Kedleston, Lord: Viceroy of India, 169, 174–7, **175**, 179–83: reforms, 176, 179; frontier policy, 180–2; and Balfour, 182; and Tibet, 181–2; clash with Kitchener, 182–3; and partition of Bengal, 183

Dalhousie, Lord, **74**, 74–5, 78
Deakin, Alfred, 126, 139, **141**
De Beers company, 151
De la Rey, General, 158
De Lesseps, Ferdinand, **109**, 110–12, 185, 190
Delhi Durbar (1903), **183**
Derby, Earl of, 126
De Rothschild, Baron, 186
De Wet, General, 158, **161**
Dilke, Sir Charles, 119, 188
Disraeli, Benjamin (Earl of Beaconsfield), 104, **116**, 148, 150, 165: purchase of Suez Canal shares, **184**, 185–6
Dost Mahommed, Amir, 70–2, 92
Doukhobors, the, 133
Dufferin, Lord, 171–2
Durham, Lord, 98: and Durham Report, 9, 18–20, **19**, 24

Edinburgh, Duke of, **117**
Egypt, 116, 184–96, 209, 211: and

Sudan, 116, 195, 201; Anglo-French financial control, 186–7; Arabi's revolt, 187–90; domestic reforms, 192; balancing of budget, 192; improved irrigation, 192
Elgin, Lord, 24, 92
Ellenborough, Lord, 72
Elles, Major-General, 182
English law and the Empire, 117–18
Esquimault harbour, **20**
Eugénie, Empress, 112
Eureka affair (1854), 37
Expansion of England (Seeley), 119
Eyre, Governor Edward John and Jamaica Rebellion, **100**, 102–4

Farewell, Lieut., 62
Fashoda incident (1898), 191, 200
Fenians, the, 12, 27
Fiji, 204, **204**
Fleming, Sir Sandford, **15**
French, Sir John, 158
Frere, Sir Bartle, 148–9
Froude, J. A., 119

Galt, (Sir) Alexander, 26
Gladstone, W. E., 190, 191: South African policies, 64, 148–9; Indian policy, 165, 166, 168; and Arabi's revolt, 188; Gordon and the Sudan, 195, 197
Gold Coast, 95, 105, 209, 211, 216
Gordon, Major-General Charles George, 195–7, **196**: chosen to supervise withdrawal from Sudan, 195–6; besieged in Khartoum, 197; relief expedition, 197, 199; killed, 197, 200
Gordon, George William, 102–4
Government of India Act (1858), 88–90
Great Trek, the (1837), **54**, 58–9, **61**, **63**, 150
Greater Britain (Dilke), 119
Grey, Third Earl, 24
Grey, Sir Edward, 11
Grey, Sir George, 46, 51, 63–4, **64**
Griqualand West, 65
Gurkhas, 81, 91

Habibulla, Amir, 181
Haldane, R. B. (Visct Haldane), 12
Harcourt, Sir William, 161
Hart, (Sir) Robert, 205
Hartington, Marquess of, 188
Hastings, Warren, 68
Havelock, Sir Henry, 84
Hermann, Captain, **208**
Hertzog, General, 158
Het Volk party (South Africa), 163
Hicks Beach, Sir Michael, 155
Hicks Pasha, 195, 197
Hinduism and Hindus, 15, 77, 79, 88, 91, 118, 178

Hobson, J. A., 210
Hofmeyer, Jan, 151, 155
Holland, Sir Henry, 116
Holtermann, Bernard, 137
Hong Kong, 204: annexed by British, 204; Happy Valley racecourse, **118**; New Territories, 204
Hottentots, the, 55, 59
Hudson Bay Company, 27, 28

Ilbert Bill (India), 169–70
Imperial defence, 120–2: colonies' contributions, 120–1
Imperial Federation League, 119
Imperial federation proposals, 125–7, 134
Imperial trade, 122–5: imperial preference, 123, 124, 134; Chamberlain and tariff reform **123**, 123–5, 134
India, 68–93, 78–81, 115, 164–83, **169**, **172**, **173**: stamps, **8**; East India Company, see separate entry; India Act (1784), 68, 166; and Afghanistan, 70–2, **166**, 166–8; annexations, 72–5, 168; Sikh Wars, **73**, 73–4; religions and cultural practice, 77–8; Government of India Act (1858), 88, 90; created an Empire (1876), 115, 165, 166; Ripon's reforms, 166; Indian National Congress, 169, 183; British investment in India, 170–1; Viceroy's office, 172–4; Curzon's viceroyalty, 174–7, 179–83; great famine (1900), **176**; untouchables, **177**; cotton industry, 178; partition of Bengal (1905), 183
Indian Civil Service, 88, 118, 166, 168, 171, 173, 213
Indian Mutiny (1857), 11, 78–84, **81**, **85**, 91, 111: British retaliation and revenge, **86**, 86–7, **87**, **89**; British and Indian reactions, 87–8
'Indirect Rule', 212–14
Iraq, 215
Ireland: famine (1845), 22, 23: continued emigration to Canada, 132; Irish Free State, 216
Isandhlwana, battle of (1879), **146**, 148
Islam, 15, 86, 178
See also Moslems
Ismail, Khedive of Egypt, **110**, 112, 113, 185–6, 196

Jamaica, 98: slavery and emancipation, 99, 101; rebellion (1865), 11, 101–4, **103**, 207; Crown Colony rule, 104, 116
Jameson, Dr (Sir) L. S., and Jameson Raid, 152–3, **152**, **153**, 155

Johannesburg, 150: railway to Delagoa Bay, 152

Kaffirs, the, 55: Kaffir War (1834–5), 57, 58
Kanakas, the, 138
Kandyan chiefs, Ceylon, **106**
Kelly, Ned, **40**, 42
Kenya, 209, 211, 216
Khahfa, the, 199, 200, **201**
Khartoum, siege of (1884–5), 197
Kiau-chau, 205
Kimberley: discovery of diamonds, 65, **146**, 147; siege of, 157, 158
Kimberley, Lord, 188 ,
Kipling, Rudyard, **117**, 161
Kitchener, Sir Herbert (Earl Kitchener of Khartoum), 199: Sirdar of Egyptian Army, **198**; in command in Sudan, 199–201; in South Africa, 57–8; clash with Curzon, 182–3
Kowloon, 204
Kruger, Paul, 149, **151**, **154**, 156, 163: and the Uitlanders, 150, 155, 156; and Jameson Raid, 155

Ladysmith, siege of, 157, 158
Laurier, Sir Wilfred, 127, **127**, 134, **135**, 136
Lawrence, Sir Henry, 74, 84
Lawrence, (Sir) John (Lord Lawrence), 74, 84, 91, **92**, 93
League of Nations mandates, 215
Letter from Sydney, A (Wakefield), 34
Livingstone, David, **96**
Lloyd George, David, 161
London, Convention of (1884), 149, 150
Lucknow, **89**: relief of, **82–3**, 84, **86**
Lugard, Lord, 213
Lytton, Earl of, 165–7, **167**, 171
Lytton, Lord, 64

Macdonald, (Sir) John, 28, **29**, 134, **135**
McNab, Sir Allan, 24
Mafeking, siege and relief of, 12, **156**, 157, 158
Mahdi, the, and Mahdism, 194–7, 199: desecration of his remains, 200
Majuba Hill, battle of (1881), 149, **149**, **151**
Malacca, 95, 106
Malaya, 96, 106, 203
Malta, 95, **121**
Manitoba, 130, **132**, 133
Maoris, 44, **44**, **45**, 46, **47**, **48**, 49–53, **53**: Second Maori War, 49, 51, 53, 120
Maps of the British Empire: 1837, **10–11**; 1901, **12–13**
Marchand, Colonel, 200, **200**

Maritz, Gerrit, 58
Matabele, the, 58
Mauritius, 95
Mayo, Lord, 165, 172
Melbourne, Lord, 18, 20
Menelek, King of Abyssinia, 199
Mennonites, the, **132**, 133
Mesopotamia, 215, 216
Mill, John Stuart, 139
Milner, Sir Alfred (Visct Milner) and 'Milnerism', **154**, 155, 156, 162
Moguls, the, 68, 70, **76**
Monserrat, 98
Montreal, 21, 23, 27, 131, 133
Morley, John, 126, 161, 188
Moslems, 77, 79, 81, 86, **87**, 91, 105, 118
See also Islam
Munro, Thomas, 68
Mwanga, Kabaka of Buganda, 210

Nana Sahib, 81
Nanking, Treaty of, 107
Napier, Sir Charles, 72–3
Napoleon III, 112
Natal, 9, 121: annexed (1843), 60; separate Crown Colony, 62
Navigation Acts repealed (1849), 10, 25
Nevis, 98
New Brunswick, 16, 24, 27–9
New Guinea, 139, 204, 215
New Hebrides, 116
'New Imperialism', 12, 14, 15
New South Wales, 17, 35, 36, 38–9, 50, 61, 137: stamps, **8**; self-government, 11, 42, **43**; and transportation of convicts, 32, 33
New Zealand, 9, 43–53, 64, 120–1, 142–5: stamps, **8**; New Zealand Company, 34–5, 45, **45**, 46; Maoris, *see* separate entry; flourishing economy, 49–50; gold strikes, 50, **51**; self-government, 11, 51–3; New Zealand Constitution Act (1852), 51–2; opts out of Australian federation, 140, 142–3; social reforms and legislation, 143–5
Newfoundland, 16, 27, 29, 130, 134: stamps, **8**
Nicholson, John, 84
Niger delta and Nigeria, 95, 209, 212
Norman, Sir Henry, and Norman Commission to West Indies, 208
North Borneo, 116, 203, 204
Northbrook, Lord, 165, 188
Northern Territory (Australia), 35
Nova Scotia, 16, 21, 27–9: responsible government, 24

Nubar Pasha, 186
Nyasaland, 116, 209

Oceana (Froude), 119
Omdurman, battle of (1898), 12, **198**, 199–200
Ontario, 16, 21, 27, 61, 130
Opium Wars, 107, **108**
Orange Free State, 60, 63–5, 147–9, 156, 160, 209: racial segregation, 62; invasion by Transvaal (1857), 63; becomes autonomous (1906), 163
Oregon, partition of, 24
Otago gold strike (1861), 50, **51**
Ottawa, 28, 29
Oudh, annexation of, 75
Overland Mail, the, 110

Palestine, 215
Palmerston, Lord, 70, 97, 108, 111
Papineau, Louis Joseph, 17, 19
Papua, 204
Parkes, Sir Henry, 126, 139
Peel, Sir Robert, 10, 97
Penang, 95, 106, 203: Diamond Jubilee arch, **124**
Persia and Afghanistan, 70, 71
Persian Gulf, 95
Peters, Carl, 209
Phillip, Governor Arthur, 31
Pitt, William. 32, 68, 166
Port Arthur, 205
Port Said, **193**
Portuguese colonies in Africa, 155
Pretoria Convention (1881), 149
Prince Edward Island, 27, 28: joins Confederation (1873), 29, 130
Protectorates, 116
Punjab, the, 70–3, 81: annexation of, 74

Quebec, 16, 17, 19, 21, 27–9, 130
Queensland, 137, 139, 140: self-government, 11, 42

Rand gold strike (1886), 36, 150
Ranjit Singh, 71–3
Red Sea, 95
Reeves, William Pember, 145
Retief, Piet, 58, 59
Rhodes, Cecil, 14, **150**, 151–3, 155, 163: British South Africa Company, 14, 151, 152; diamond and gold companies, 151; Prime Minister of Cape Colony, 151, 153, 155; and Jameson Raid, 152–3, 155
Rhodesia, 116, 151, 162: Northern and Southern, 209
Ripon, Lord, **167**, 168
Ritchie, C. T., 124
Roberts, Lord, 7, 157–8, 168
Robinson, Sir Hercules, 137
Rose (Sir) Hugh (Lord Strathnairn), 84
Rosebery, Earl of, 11, 197

Russell, Lord John (Earl Russell), 18

St Eustache, battle of (1837), 18
St Helena, 95
St Kitts, 98
Salisbury, Marquess of, 122, 126, 127, 155, 165, 168, 197, 199, 209, 211
Sand River Convention (1852), 60
Sarawak, 106–7, 203, 204
Saskatchewan, 130, 133
Seddon, Richard, 127, 144, 145
Seeley, Sir John, 119
Seymour, (Sir) Beauchamp, 189
Shah Shuja, 70, 72
Shanghai, 205
Shepstone, (Sir) Theophilus, 148
Sher Ali, 93
Sher Singh, 73
Sierra Leone, 95, **96**, 105
Sikhs, the, **69**, 70–4, 91: Sikh Wars, **73**, 73–4
Simla, 172, **174**
Simonstown naval base, **56**, 162
Sind, 70, **70**: annexation, 72–3
Singapore, 95–6, 106, 203, 204
Sioux Indians, **23**
Smuts, General Jan, 158, 163
Somaliland, 209
South Africa, 54–67, 139, 146–63, 215: Kaffir War, 57, 58: abolition of slavery, 57–8; Great Trek, see separate entry; question of federation, 63, 64; diamond rush, 65, **146**, 147; farming prosperity, 65–6; life in towns, 66–7; Zulu War (1879), **146**, 148; South African War (1880–1), 149, **149**; South African War (1899–1902), see separate entry; Customs union (1903), 162; Union of South Africa (1910), 163
See also under separate colonies
South African War (1899–1902), 12, 14, 122, 134, 156–62, **156**, **157**, **159**: 'black week', 157; fall of Pretoria, 158; campaign by Boer commandos, 158, **161**, **162**; farm-burning and concentration camps, 160, **160**
South Australia: South Australian Company, 34–5; self-government, 11, 42
South-west Africa, 215
Spithead Review (1897), **119**
Stephen, Sir James, 60, 97
Sudan, the, 139, 191, 194–201, 209: the Mahdi and Mahdism, 194–7; siege of Khartoum, 197; campaign of 1896–9, 156, 198–200; condominium, 116, 201; Civil Service, 201, 213
Suez Canal, 109–13, **111**, 185–6, 190, 192–4, 211; de Lesseps'

project, 110–11; British opposition and French support, 111–12; opening of Canal, 112–13, **113**, 185; Disraeli buys Khedive's shares, 185–6; Convention (1888), 191
Suttee (widow-burning), 77, 78
Swazi, the, 58
Sydenham, Lord, 24

Tanganyika, **208**, 209, 215
Tariff reform, **123**, 123–5, 134
Tasmania, 35, 137: and transportation of convicts, 32, 33; aborigines, 39; self-government, 11, 42
Tel-el-Kebir, battle of, 189–90
Tewfik, Khedive of Egypt, 186–90
Thugs, the, 78
Tibet: Curzon's policy, 181; Younghusband's expedition (1903–4), 182
Togoland, 215
Tonga, 116, 204
Toronto, 21, 23, 27, 131, 133
Transjordan, 215
Transvaal, 12, 60, 63, 64, 160, 163, 209: racial segregation, 62; farming prosperity, 65; British annexation (1877), 148, 150; war of 1880–1, 149, **149**; independence, 149; question of suzerainty, 149; Rand gold strike (1899), 36, 150; Uitlanders, 150–4; Jameson Raid, 152–3, 155; outbreak of war (1899), 156; autonomy (1906), 162–3
Trincomalee naval base, 105
Trinidad, 98, 116, **207**
Tristan da Cunha, **94**, 95
Tz'u Hsi, Dowager Empress, 206

Uganda, 116, 197, 209, 212: Indian labour, **210**
Uitlanders, the, 150–3, **152**, 155–6: Jameson Raid, 152–3, 155; full citizenship, 163
Ulundi, battle of, 148
Uys, Jacobus, 58

Van Dieman's Land, see Tasmania
Vancouver and Vancouver Island, 24, 27, 133
Vereenigring, Peace of (1902), 160
Victoria, 17, 35, 38–9, 41, 50: gold rush, 35–6; self-government, 11, 42
Victoria, Queen, 9, 85, **116**, 127, 185–6, 200: Empress of India, 117, 165, 166; and death of Gordon, 197; Golden Jubilee (1887), 120, 127; Diamond Jubilee (1897), **119**, **124**, 127, 134
Vogel, (Sir) Julius, 145

Waghorn, Thomas, 110
Waitangi, Treaty of (1840), 46, **47**, 52
Wakefield, Edward Gibbon, 9, 18, 34–5, **35**, 43–4
Watkins, Edward, 28
Wei-hai-Wei, 204, **213**
Wellesley, Richard (Marquess Wellesley), 68, 70
West Indies, see British West Indies
Western Australia, 32, 35, 42: responsible government (1893), 139–40
Wilhelm II, Kaiser, telegram to Kruger, 155
Winnipeg, **131**
Wolseley, (Sir Garnet) (Visct Wolseley), 85–6: and battle of Tel-el-Kebir, 189–90; commands Gordon relief expedition, 197
Wood, Sir Evelyn, **151**

Yakub, Amir, 167, 168
York, Duke of (King George V), **142**
Younghusband, Col (Sir Francis), 182

Zanzibar, 209: Sultan of, 95
Zionist movement, 212
Zulu, the, 58, **62**, 147: Zulu War (1879), **146**, 148